THE
BROKEN
ROAD

THE BROKEN ROAD

(A Mother's Journey)

PAIGE WALKER

To order additional copies of this book, contact:
Xlibris Corporation
0-800-891-366
www.xlibris.co.nz
Orders@ Xlibris.co.nz
700096

Preface

This is a true account of my struggle as a mother of a sexually abused child and its effects on me as a mother and a woman. Many accounts have been documented of the atrocities inflicted upon our young children, but little is known or documented of the effect it has on the mother and family as a whole.

This book took on a life of its own when I started writing a journal of my daughter's disclosure and became my catharsis. Its true creation came about after I discovered a lack of support for parents in the community, which, as I wrote, grew into a passionate desire to acknowledge and validate the struggle for parents who have to endure the aftermath and devastating effects the abuse has on their child and themselves.

I hope that when you finish reading this book, you will truly believe that one day you will get through this and that even during your darkest moments, as I did, you will call upon your inner strength to see you through to the next day.

If this account of my journey into the abyss touches and comforts even one mother, then it was worth writing.

My hope is that one day society will recognise the devastating effects child sexual abuse has on our mothers and that more appropriate support systems are put into place to support and counsel these women through this harrowing experience.

Life is never the same again after a child's disclosure, but with love, professional guidance, and community support, life can become bearable once more, though the scars and memories will always remain.

Paige Walker

Thank you for reading and walking this broken road with me. I hope that you find some measure of comfort knowing you do not have to endure this pain alone. You are not alone as I too have walked in your shoes, and many mothers before us and many more after us will walk this same journey.

Paige Walker
Auckland, New Zealand, 2011

Chapter 1

5 June 2009

The day of my daughter's disclosure was the day I died, 5 June 2009. It was a typical Friday night, my daughter and I were just settling down to watch the final of New Zealand's Next Top Model: from the beginning of the series we had both been rooting for Chrystabelle; with minutes to spare to the opening credits, my daughter grabbed my hand, placed it on her crotch, and said,

'Let's have some fun, Mummy!'

She then placed her tiny fingers on my private parts and proceeded to tickle me with one hand while the other hand swiftly tried to slide into my underwear, all the while giggling at the prospect of her interpretation of fun with me totally unaware of the chaos and devastation about to be unleashed in that inconceivably inappropriate action towards me.

It didn't sink in at first; my immediate reaction was to scold her saying,

'We don't do things like that.'

I reprimanded her as Tyra Banks danced across the TV screen; then slowly, as the seconds ticked by, the realisation hit me like a ton of bricks. My heart was pounding so hard against my rib cage that I thought it would jump out at me. My mind raced as I tried to unscramble my thoughts. I knew I had to ask her the hard questions that were accumulating in my head.

'Oh god no.' I was crying inside. I couldn't think straight. I was sweating profusely! I couldn't let her see my distress, I had to calm down and collect myself.

Looking straight into her eyes, I asked her.

Paige Walker

'*Has somebody touched you down there?*'

First of all, she said no, but I knew my daughter so well that I knew she was lying and scared. We had a golden rule at home that as long as she told me the truth, no matter what or how bad it was or how much trouble she was in, I would never be angry or mad at her. The important thing is that she tells me the truth, so I asked her again.

Maybe the children at school had been messing around as some of them were at that prepubescent stage, I thought.

I just about died when she whispered his name.

Maybe I didn't hear her clearly as my brain tried to reason with me, but she quietly repeated his name again.

A flood of emotions hit me all at once; I couldn't breathe. I was shaking in disbelief, but yet a part of me knew it to be true.

My beautiful daughter has been sexually abused by a trusted family friend.

As I listened to my daughter, a Tsunami of emotions rolled over me.

Shock, horror, anger, and numbness crashed down on me as the reality of her words hit home.

Tyra and the two remaining contestants were battling it out in the finals, while inside, I was battling to hold it together.

'*Don't you believe me, Mummy?*' she asked with a desperate look in her eyes!

'*Oh! Baby! Yes, Mummy believes you. You are such a brave girl to tell me.*'

As I cradled her in my arms, I heard this tiny voice, full of desperation and fear, cry out,

'*Do you still love me?*'

I looked at her, so small, so vulnerable!

'*Mummy will always love you.*'

'*I was scared to tell you,*' she claimed as her tears of relief flowed freely.

As we held each other in a tight embrace, I promised her nobody would ever hurt her again! She thanked me saying she felt much better now for telling me.

Tears stung at the back of my eyes.

'*Why is she thanking me?*' I thought to myself.

I had let her down, I had failed her as a mother, I didn't protect her, and I wasn't there for her when she needed me.

I paced the room frantically, for one of only a few times in my life I didn't know what to do, and I felt completely and totally helpless.

I needed to talk to somebody.

Thoughts of the local vicar crossed my mind.

My daughter had always been very religious. Baptised a Catholic in the family church, she always attended Sunday Mass with Grandma when we lived in the UK, and since being in New Zealand, she attended the local church, which ran the Sunday Bible study group for primary school-aged children.

She read her Bible and said her prayers before bed every night. While I was keen to encourage her faith, I never shared that same belief. Raised a Catholic myself, I had some very strong opinions about Christ and God; however, I never imposed my beliefs upon her.

She attended church on a regular basis and went to Bible study.

The local vicar had been troubled about my lack of faith and attendance at church and had always tried to corner me at any opportunity she got to discuss it with me. The previous week she had called by our house unannounced, inconveniently, at dinner time, just as we were settling down to eat. Not wanting to be rude, I arranged a coffee meeting with her for the following week. She had me well and truly cornered now; this time I couldn't avoid her.

It was so ironic that, after months of trying to avoid her, that very afternoon of my daughter's disclosure, she had managed to catch me for a coffee and an informal session on where I was with my faith, and now it was her that I turned to.

I sat with my daughter and explained to her how mummy needed to talk to another adult about what she had just told me.

Still reeling from the shock of her disclosure, I called the vicarage, not even sure if the vicar would be in as I knew she had a bach up north and went there most weekends to prepare her sermon for the Sunday service. (A bach is a small holiday home or beach house commomly used in New Zealand.) As the dial tone connected, I said a silent prayer to myself, *'Please be in,'* but it was answered by her husband. I steadied my voice the best I could and asked to speak with her; as he put the phone down and called out for her, the dead space between the two phone lines haunted me. When she picked up, I briefly outlined what had just transpired that evening, struggling to keep it together emotionally, and asked if I could call by as I needed someone to talk to.

I don't know how I managed to drive over to the vicarage that night; it was only a five-minute drive by car from our place, but it felt like forever as if time had stood still. I dropped my daughter off at the church house with one of the youth leaders and asked if she could look after my daughter while I had a meeting with the vicar.

I had thought ahead and brought my daughter's colouring books with us to keep her occupied. It was funny how even in a crisis, I had remembered such a trivial item; my world had fallen apart around me, yet I had the foresight to remember her colouring books!

Paige Walker

As I walked up the cobbled path to the vicarage, I noticed her car parked in the driveway. Still feeling rattled from our coffee morning, I approached her house with trepidation, unsure how I would be received after my upfront and personal revelations with her that afternoon. I paused a moment outside the front door, trying to compose myself before entering and then rang the bell. I could hear the chimes reverberating, as my arrival was announced.

Opening the door, she warmly invited me in where I spent the next two hours reliving my nightmare: the first of many accounts.

Chapter 2

I started my nursing career in 1984 as a pupil nurse in the UK, at the age of seventeen and a half.

After a two-year course, I qualified as an Enrolled Nurse, but I soon came to realise that my passion was working alongside children. I then applied for the Registered Sick Children's Nursing course at the University of Manchester, and after three arduous years, I qualified as a Registered Nurse with a Diploma in Paediatric Nursing Studies.

I first came to New Zealand (Aotearoa, the Maori name for New Zealand translated as 'land of the long white cloud') in 1999, for a short period of time on a twelve-month working holiday contract, working at StarShip Children's Hospital. With twenty years of experience, I was a highly qualified, experienced nurse, with specialised skills in paediatric medicine and general nursing. I was blessed with a job that I loved, excelled at, which also challenged my passionate and caring nature.

During that time I met a Samoan guy, whom I fell madly in love with. We dated for over ten months, when unexpectedly, I found myself pregnant.

The news of my condition didn't go down as well as I expected, and I soon found myself alone, pregnant and very scared! With no family or support in New Zealand, I had no choice but to return home to the UK, leaving my heart in New Zealand.

My daughter was three years old when we both returned to New Zealand in search of a better life. We fell in love with the people, the laid-back lifestyle, and considered New Zealand our home.

We settled on the North Shore and embraced the Kiwi lifestyle, which included frequent days out on the beach, Christmas in the sun, and becoming diehard All

Paige Walker

Blacks rugby supporters. With routines established with school, work, and friends, we enjoyed our lives to the fullest.

As a dual-qualified nurse, I worked for a temping agency and work was plentiful. I worked within a wide range of nursing areas, enhancing my skill-based practice and increasing my nursing knowledge along the way. Back in 2005, I was asked to do a night shift on the maternity ward. I was not a midwife and had no experience in midwifery, other than giving birth to my daughter, so with apprehension, I accepted the shift.

It was a busy night, with newborn babies to feed and change, assisting the mothers with difficult babies; the mothers themselves exhausted after just given birth, the night went fast! I ended my shift on a high that morning and never looked back.

For two years I worked exclusively on the maternity ward, loving every minute of it, until I sustained a wrist injury one night, in November 2007.

Breastfeeding is highly promoted on the ward as babys best food however there are times when mothers are unable to breastfed therefore hand expressing is performed. Hand expressing is a technique used to aid mothers to manually express their breast milk. I had been taught by a senior midwife and performed the task previously on numerous occasions, so why on this particular night, I don't know, but while assisting a new mother expressing, I experienced a sharp pain radiating up my left wrist towards my elbow. Thinking I might have overworked or strained it, I swapped hands, and the same thing happened to my right wrist. The pain was so intense that I became dizzy and nauseous and needed to sit down.

I struggled to get through the rest of that night; every nursing task I performed brought on a new wave of pain.

The following morning I took myself off to the physiotherapy clinic where I was diagnosed with *bilateral De Quervain's, in both wrists* and placed in splints.

De Quervain's is an inflammation of the tendon and sheath in the wrist caused by intense and continuous use, and the only option at this stage was to rest them in splints, and an ACC form was completed.

Accident Compensation Corporation (ACC) is a corporation, which provides no-fault-personal-injury-compensation cover for all New Zealand residents and visitors to New Zealand. The earners scheme is funded from levies paid by employers on wages paid to employees and also from levies paid by self-employed people. As I qualified under the earners scheme, I was sent home with strict instructions to rest. I knew I wouldn't be able to go back to work that night, and so following a visit to my GP for a medical certificate, I was signed off sick for three weeks.

Unbeknown at the time, that I would be off work indefinitely, as a cruel twist of fate awaited me.

My wrists never recovered. From then onwards, I was subjected to steroid injections, on two separate occasions, I had X-rays done and ultrasound scans performed, and as the inflammation in both wrists never settled down, I started having weekly physiotherapy sessions too, but nothing seemed to work.

I was wearing my splints daily, which was a constant source of frustration for me as they limited my range of hand movement, but I tried to keep a sense of normality around my daughter, and that's when I had my fall!

It was the middle of summer; beautiful blue skies graced us every morning when we awoke, and the heat of the burning sun danced over our bodies, bronzing us to a rich golden brown; we both looked healthy and full of life with our tans.

My daughter was fortunate to have received a bike from the *Variety*, 'Bikes for Kids' programme when they nominated North Shore children that year.

Each year Variety provides around 450 deserving or disadvantaged children with the freedom and independence of their very own bike on their 'Bikes for Kids Tour'; my daughter was one of the children nominated.

One afternoon that summer, my daughter wanted to go to the park to ride her bike. As soon as we arrived at Marlborough Park, in Glenfield, she grabbed her bike and took off around the cycle path, leaving me to gather up the camping chairs and picnic basket from the car boot, not forgetting my book, to secure my spot under the shade of the trees. I always had a sense of serenity when reading outdoors; I found it very therapeutic.

Exhausted after a few rounds on the cycle path, my daughter wanted to play catch. Saving the page where I was reading in my book, I jumped up, ready and eager to play with her.

We had a good volley going, with no missed catches. When suddenly she aimed the ball a few feet short of where I was standing, I lunged forward, unwilling to be the one to drop the ball first, when unexpectedly I tripped and found myself plunging towards the ground. My wrists still in soft splints, I instinctively drew my wrists up to my chest to protect them, which resulted in me landing full weight onto my right shoulder.

Pain ripped through my shoulder joint as I tried to get up; then and there I knew immediately I had damaged something. This earned me another visit to physiotherapy and another ACC form.

Paige Walker

I was diagnosed with a bursitis, an inflammation of a bursa, which is a small fluid filled sac-like structure mainly found surrounding joints. After a period of rest and immobility, the pain hadn't subsided, and a steroid injection was administered into my shoulder joint with little effect. The first year passed, and I was still off work. I had had multiple examinations by various doctors; a further two steroid injections were given in my right shoulder, which still didn't help, and by that time, I was begging for surgery on both my wrists and shoulder as I was in so much pain, but still ACC continued to subject me to further tests and examinations. Finally, I was seen by an orthopaedic surgeon, who diagnosed an AC joint shoulder injury within seconds. At last, I had some answers, and surgery was quickly arranged. Not long after that, I was seen by a hand and wrist specialist, and as I had exhausted all other avenues of treatment, surgery was also recommended.

Thank God! Now all I had to do was to wait for funding and approval by ACC for both surgeries.

Chapter 3

I reflect back on the ill-fated meeting and of the friendship with this man, and his family, who had abused my daughter's trust, which turned our lives upside down, every minute wishing that I could turn back the clock. In December 2007, my mother came to New Zealand for an extended visit, so we decided to do an eleven-day *Tiki Tour* of the North Island.

New Zealand is such a beautiful country that I wanted to explore more of what it had to offer.

Travelling is in my blood, with my father being in the British Army, we were never in one place long enough to call home.

I had travelled the world pre-motherhood, from Canada, the Bahamas to Hong Kong, Singapore, and beyond. Excited, we planned our route.

We left Auckland and headed to Mount Maunganui in Tauranga situated in the Bay of Plenty. The Bay of Plenty was given its name when Captain Cook circumnavigated New Zealand in 1769.

The drive there was uneventful. While Mum and I marvelled at the scenery, my daughter watched movies on her portable DVD player that she received for Christmas, purposely bought, with the trip in mind.

On arrival at Papamoa Holiday Resort, we checked in only to find our self-contained apartment was right on the beach front. Fantastic! It was so perfect!

Lying in bed that night, we all drifted off to sleep with the lull of gentle waves cascading onto the sandy shores.

After a good night's sleep, we drove across to the East Coast, stopping overnight in Napier, and then down to Wellington, New Zealand's capital.

Arriving at the Top Ten Holiday Park, my daughter took off to the playground where children were already playing, while Mum and I unloaded the car as we were staying there for three nights. It didn't take long for my daughter to come back, looking for food as she was always hungry; no matter how much she ate, she was always looking for some snack or another. However, it wasn't just her on the doorstep; she had brought along two little girls she had befriended at the playground.

She proudly introduced Natalia and Anna to me, grabbed some chips, and scooted off again with the girls in tow. One thing about my daughter, she always managed to find a friend, no matter where she was. She had oodles of confidence and would quite happily go over and talk to other children. It was a strong characteristic of hers, one in which I was surely lacking!

Having unpacked, Mum and I settled down on the deck with a well-earned cup of tea.

Mum and I never needed an excuse for a cuppa; the kettle was permanently switched on; I guess that was one of the very few English traits I identified with. With my daughter in sight, playing with the girls, a cuppa cradled in my hand, I reflected on my life and how good things were.

The girls were back and wanted to watch TV; we had *SKY TV* in our apartment, which, to us was a luxury, I could never afford at home. I suggested to the girls that while it was OK to stay, they had better go and tell their parents where they were. It was one of my golden rules I had instilled in my daughter, that she must always let me know where she was at all times. I had visions of this poor mother roaming round the resort grounds scared and in fear for her offspring's lives. I know New Zealand is often described as God's country but still stuff happens (little did I know at the time that, that thought was to haunt me for the rest of my life). Off they all scurried, and as soon as they left, they were back with squeals of laughter and said, *'It's OK with Mum.'* They settled down in front of the TV while Mum and I decided what was on the menu for dinner that evening.

The Disney channel was blaring in the background; that's why I never heard the call at first, but I did notice a Pacific Island woman dressed in a beautiful Hawaiian-print Muumuu dress outside our apartment.

'This must be the girls' mother,' I thought. I went outside introduced myself then called for the girls.

It appeared that they were from Auckland too but were in Wellington for their sister's wedding, and that evening they were heading out for dinner, so with the usual moans and protests of children being torn away from whatever fun activity that they were involved in, and with the promise of meeting up and playing together the next day, they left, and we settled down for the evening.

The following day I wanted to take Mum on the *Beehive Tour* that I had done on a previous visit to Wellington with an old friend. (The Beehive is the common name of the New Zealand Parliament Buildings. It is so-called because its shape is reminiscent of that of a traditional woven form of beehive known as a skep.)

We got there too early for the next available tour or too late, as one had already started, depending on how you view these things, but for us, it was a great opportunity to take some photos and some video footage outside the Beehive. With my handycam at hand, we went on a look-see around the grounds, which were stunning!

Statues of previous prime ministers and important dignitaries dotted the grounds amongst the beautiful and colourful array of flowers. Mum, with her green fingers, correctly identified their individual species; while I appreciated her commentary, to me, they were just beautiful flowers there for our visual pleasure.

Time passed really quickly, and it was soon time to head up to the main entrance where we were escorted into the main lobby to be seated and await our tour guide. I was feeling excited for Mum as I remembered being quite impressed on my first visit.

The tour guide arrived and started her spiel of dos and dont's, location of toilets, fire exits, etc, and not forgetting the souvenir shop on the way out.

We started off in the lobby and moved round the Beehive at a snail's pace, but surprisingly, I found myself engaged with the guide and enjoying myself.

Suddenly my daughter wrestled her hand out of mine and took off after two little girls she had spotted amongst the crowd. It was the two girls she had been playing with yesterday in the play area at the holiday park. One was holding onto her mother's hand, whom I had already met, while the other was with an older gentleman I presumed was their grandfather. We didn't speak to the adults though the girls spent the rest of the tour together, giggling and talking non-stop. As the tour guide was coming to the end of the tour, we quietly left the building in search of something to eat, as it was way past lunchtime, and we were all hungry. Our search found us outside Burger King, and we headed upstairs. Not long after we sat down with our meals, we heard the sound of laughter coming from the stairwell. As heads appeared over the railings, my daughter screamed in delight as the girls we had just met at the Beehive, their mother, and presumed grandfather arrived.

Paige Walker

'*Are you guys following us?*' I commented in jest.

I invited them to join us at our table where we made our introductions: I, Mum, and my daughter, and the Blackwell family, Cameron, Mia, and the girls, Natalia and Anna. My mouth must have dropped to the floor when Cameron announced he was the girls' father! I was so shocked!

He must have been well into his early 60s, not that age is a factor with men and procreation, it's a well-known fact that men can have children well into their twilight years. I guess the age difference was just so apparent! After I picked my jaw up off the floor, we all chatted with an ease of familiarity.

They had been in Wellington a few days ahead of us and recommended a few tourist sights, while I appreciated their suggestions I had already planned our agenda for the few days that we were there. As they were leaving for Auckland the next day, the girls made promises to meet in the playground that evening to exchange phone numbers as they wanted to meet up when we got home. I remember at the time feeling pleased that my daughter had made some friends, they appeared to be a loving family, the girls got on really well, and it wouldn't hurt my daughter to have some more friends of her own age as she already spent too much time with me and other adult company.

As soon as they left, we also departed and headed up towards the *Wellington Cable Car*. (*The Wellington Cable Car* is one of Wellington's oldest and most popular tourist attractions. At the top, it has magnificent views overlooking the city and the harbour.) The rest of our day was spent browsing around the shops.

There was so much to see and do in Wellington, but the highlight definitely was *Te Papa*, New Zealand's National Museum: we spent the next day there, where we all learnt so much about New Zealand's heritage and culture.

The following morning, we left Wellington and headed up the west coast towards New Plymouth, passing through Manaia, near Wanganui, famous for its bread and then on to Waitomo Caves to see the Glowworms which was our final stop before home.

Chapter 4

After twelve days on the road, it was good to be home. My daughter wanted to call the girls as soon as we arrived, but I told her to wait till the weekend.

Normal life resumed and the next few months were busy; my daughter was back at school, and Mum had already left.

After making contact with the Blackwell family, my daughter and I started spending more and more weekends with them, going out on day trips or just hanging out together. Sometimes Cameron would come along but mostly it was Mia, myself, and the three girls. We attended the Easter Show, which was a first for us, movies, and each other's birthday parties; the girls, by this time, had developed a strong friendship. Yes, there were squabbles, fights, and the occasional tears with girls being girls, but on the whole, they got on really well.

Then the sleepovers started.

If I was to be honest, I was truly grateful for them. A weekend by myself was pure heaven; being a single parent, there was never enough time in the day for *me* time; a quick hour, snatched here and there during the day was about it for me, so I welcomed the break.

Around about September 2008, my daughter's behaviour started changing. It was very subtle at first, nothing to indicate anything out of the norm; she was growing up, maturing, but then her attitude towards me became very hostile, and I couldn't quite understand why. There were tantrums and tears and some major meltdowns. She started lying and stealing, which frustrated me as she had just about everything she needed and wanted and was very much loved; there was just no need for it, but nothing seemed right any more. I had recently

21

told her about her absent father. Surprisingly, she had handled that quite well; so I thought.

The existence of her father never came up in conversation until Father's Day in September 2008 when she came home from school with a Mother's Day card. As she explained to me that all the children in her class had made Father's Day cards, but as she didn't have a dad, she made me a Mother's Day card, instead, because she didn't want to feel left out. I was so overwhelmed with guilt, that, that afternoon, I sat her down and told her about the father she never knew she had.

'Was her difficult behaviour, resentment and anger towards me, a result of that?' I questioned myself.

I didn't believe so, but I wasn't entirely sure.

My daughter was usually very loud, opinionated, and vocal, but our relationship had always been a very loving one; however, recently we weren't connecting on an emotional level. Some psychologists would argue that as I never breastfed her, so we never bonded from birth: that argument I would strongly dispute. Millions of children around the world were raised on formula and are very well adjusted. It was just her nature.

'She was becoming very much like me in a way, the strong independent silent type.' So I thought.

But her behaviour became more and more troublesome. It started off with faecal smearing all over the toilet seat and bathroom walls and the onset of bed-wetting. There were episodes of overeating: suddenly she developed a lack of interest in activities she previously enjoyed and, instead of her usual bubbly self, became introverted and clingy. I leant on Mia for moral support and help. Mia was willing to have my daughter on the occasional weekends to give me a break, so I allowed her to have more frequent visits and sleepovers.

I was soon becoming desperate and frustrated as every time I tried to engage my daughter in conversation about her feelings, all I got from her was that she was fine, or if I asked how her day was at school, all I got was a grunt or a groan: she wouldn't open up and talk to me, and I couldn't take much more of her challenging behaviour.

Every morning became a battle of verbal onslaught until she was dropped off at school, only for it to resume on her return.

The final straw came one morning, after an argument; while I was in the shower, she called the police to come and get her. I was livid! After the school run, I came home to find the police waiting for me on my doorstep. I was beside myself with anger and fear.

Not long ago, the *Anti-Smacking Law* had been passed through parliament. Although most parents don't abuse their children, unfortunately some do, and it is a big problem here in New Zealand. Although I hadn't touched her, the fear of CYFS (Children Youth and Family Services) taking her off me was very real. I was an emotional wreck, the police came in, and I was interviewed.

Amongst the tears, fears, and frustration, I explained to the police officer my delicate situation with my daughter, putting her behaviour down to the recent shock of knowing about her father.

The police officer, bless him, was a Manchester lad, from the UK, a Northern-bred Mancunian like myself, with a family of his own, and understood the difficulties, raising children. I immediately warmed to him and kept apologising profusely for my never-ending flood of tears. He suggested if there may be someone my daughter could stay with for a few days so I had some time to calm down and she had time to cool off. I immediately thought of my friend Megan. Megan is a pre-school teacher, whom I had met soon after my arrival in New Zealand in late 1994; when I enrolled my daughter into her pre-school we got on immediately and have remained friends since. I called her up at work, and after a quick explanation, she agreed to have my daughter for a few days. So that day, after school, I dropped my daughter off. I knew that, that wasn't going to be enough; she would come home after a few days away, and we would start up again. I felt I had to do something more. *I needed help!*

But I felt ashamed to need any form of professional help. I was the caregiver, the nurturing one, the strength others turned too. I was most comfortable as the carer, not the patient/client, but I was left with no options.

I called Barnardos, who organised for a social worker to call by within the next few days.

That's when I first met Cathy.

Cathy was a voluptuous lady with a bubbly personality to match. She was beautifully dressed, with matching outfits and immaculately polished nails.

Some women just had it together; unfortunately, I wasn't one of them, still sporting my tomboyish ways, living in jeans and sneakers.

I sat with Cathy for hours and explained the difficult situation with my daughter that had led to this intervention as she listened with sincere concern and understanding. I knew then that I had made the right decision in asking for help.

At that first meeting, we formulated a plan of action together, where she would meet with my daughter for a one-on-one session, first to obtain her perspective on things at home and in her life, then to work alongside us setting up some rules and boundaries, with weekly follow-ups until we reached our goals.

This went on for about ten months with hardly any improvement. We implemented different strategies, sticker books, reward charts, positive re-enforcement techniques, but one by one the behavioural change strategies failed. We then tried other approaches, but in spite of all that input, her behaviour worsened! Around the same time, Barnardos were running a parenting course, which I attended, picking up valuable parenting skills, but nothing seemed to work. Cathy and I were both at a loss, and I became more and more stressed, emotionally, mentally, and physically.

Chapter 5

ACC approved both surgeries, and my shoulder surgery was fast approaching, booked for 3 April 2009. As it was an overnight stay; it had been arranged that my daughter was to stay with Leanne over at the church house for the weekend so I could have some rest post-surgery. My daughter also would not miss out on her Bible study. Leanne was her Sunday school teacher, whom I had befriended earlier that year, and we became very close friends. She adored my daughter, and this was reciprocated. Leanne was the big sister she had always wanted. I knew my daughter was in safe hands with her.

My shoulder surgery went well; my pain levels were tolerable as long as my shoulder rested in the sling provided, and I kept it immobile. Megan picked me up from the hospital the morning of my discharge, where we stopped by the pharmacy for my prescription and then by the church as I wanted to see my daughter before being dropped off at home.

The first few days following surgery, the Blackwell family and friends passed by, even Cathy called in. I was exhausted, tired out by the constant flow of well-wishers and phone calls. In the days that followed, I soon settled down into my rehabilitation routine of daily exercises and twice-weekly physiotherapy.

My shoulder recovered relatively quickly, but driving was still an issue for me. The coming weekend was Easter break, and I had arranged with Mia for my daughter to spend it with their family while I rested. They picked her up on the Thursday afternoon after school closed and returned with her Easter Monday evening, so she could get ready for school, which resumed the next day. During those few days while my daughter was away, I stayed at home, relaxed, and caught up with some much-needed rest.

Paige Walker

The following month was my daughter's eighth birthday. We all had tickets to the Disney Princess on Ice Tour at the Vectra Arena. Mia had bought the tickets so we could sit together, and instead of me paying her back for our tickets, Il Divo were playing in October of that year, therefore I purchased tickets for the Il Divo concert for us to go together. The plan was that Mia and I were to have a girls' night out, at the concert, followed by drinks in the casino at the Sky Tower, and maybe a flutter or two, while Cameron babysit the girls. I loved the atmosphere in the casino, the buzz, the thrill of anticipation of winning the big one makes the casino the main feature of the Sky Tower. It's the tallest man-made structure in the Southern Hemisphere standing at 328m (1,076 ft) tall and has the most amazing views of the city and harbour. It also boasts New Zealand's only revolving restaurant which does a complete 360 degree rotation once every hour, dinner and the casino is a girls ultimate night out, and I couldn't wait!

The afternoon of the Disney Princess on Ice Tour, as I still wasn't able to drive after my surgery, Cameron, Mia, and the girls picked us up, so we all went together.

On arrival at the Vectra Arena, a large crowd had already assembled outside the main entrance. The girls were excited as we made our way towards the usher with tickets in hand. As we settled into our respective seats, you could literally feel the atmosphere charged with thousands of children beautifully dressed up as their favourite Disney characters, Snow Whites, Tinkerbelles, Cinderellas, and Belles dotted throughout the Arena, with a few Prince Charmings and Aladdins sandwiched amongst them.

The night was a hit with the children and adults alike.

Chapter 6

The Friday night of my daughter's disclosure is a night I will never forget.

I just about died when she whispered his name.

I thought she said Cameron, but maybe I didn't hear her correctly; she quietly whispered his name again.

After my discussion about my daughter's disclosure with the vicar that evening, I instinctively thought of Cathy. I needed her more now than the past ten months put together. I grabbed my phone, while at the back of my mind I already knew she wouldn't be available. It was late Friday night, past normal working hours, Cathy would be at home with her family, most likely curled up on her sofa, relaxing with a glass of wine. But there was always a slim chance that she might have her work phone switched on nearby.

I dialled her number.

It went straight to voicemail.

My heart sank. I needed to talk to someone else. I really wanted to talk to Cathy!

I dialled again thinking I might have dialled incorrectly in haste. Her voice floated back at me as her recording played in my ear. Disconnecting the phone with frustration, I then redialled Cathy's number and left a desperate message for her to call me back ASAP.

I tried to keep the weekend as normal as possible as I didn't want my daughter to see my distress.

I was on edge. I felt close to exploding! About 101 conflicting emotions bounced off each other like a kaleidoscope of colours, changing one after another. Instead of a ray of beauty, left behind was mayhem and confusion; it felt so unreal! I spent the remainder of the next day and night in a restless turmoil.

The following day, Sunday afternoon, my daughter had been invited to a friend's birthday party, which up until then had been an exciting prospect and she was looking forward to going but announced that morning that she didn't want to attend. Deep down, I didn't want her to go either. I just wanted to hold and protect her, shielding her from the cold cruel world outside, but it was too late for that: she had already been thrown into the adult world years beyond her age and comprehension. It was almost like shutting the barn door after the horse has bolted! *I felt so helpless!*

I encouraged her to go as all her friends were going and it would be fun, the party food, games, and laughter would serve as a great distraction for her as I felt it important to carry on as normal. After much persuasion, she got ready. I was very attentive, more than usual, with her dressing and attire. She looked adorable, and my heart just melted, tears stung my eyes threatening to overflow as I tightly squeezed them shut, in the hope of stemming the flow.

With my daughter at the party, I had a couple of hours to sit down and think; to absorb it all, it felt so surreal. In the background, the phone rang. I was tempted to leave it as I couldn't deal with any of my friend's woes or mindless gossip right now, but the ringing was relentless, irritating me, someone was desperately trying to get in touch.

'Oh my god! Cathy!' I suddenly thought as I ran to pick it up! But it was the vicar, whom I had spoken with on Friday night. Trying to keep the disappointment from my voice I answered.

'Have you reported it to the police?' she asked.

Oh my gosh! I was so anxious and distracted, trying to get hold of Cathy; in my panicked state, it never even crossed my mind. I remembered the colouring books on Friday night but didn't think of calling the police!

As soon as I hung up with her, with trembling hands and a thumping heart I dialled the emergency number 111.

'Police, ambulance or fire?' the voice at control asked.

My mind went blank!

'Hello? Police. ambulance or fire?'

'Err, pause, *err . . . Police,'* I stuttered to the controller as the line was connected and immediately answered,

'I need to talk to someone about my daughter. She has been sexually abused,' I stated.

A barrage of questions soon followed. I answered as best as I could, but my thought processes were impaired, the shock, now settling in.

'Why are you just reporting it now if your daughter disclosed this on Friday?' he asked with a judgemental tone to his voice!

I was so upset by his statement, how *dare* he talk to me with such contempt. Yes, I guess I should have called the police sooner, but the shock of it all unbalanced me. I was on a rollercoaster of emotions, and I couldn't get off, so excuse me for being human!

'OK, an officer will be with you just after 7 p.m.' he replied.

My daughter was due to be picked up from the party at 6.30 p.m. I didn't want her in the house while the police officers were present; she'd been through enough this past forty-eight hours, and I didn't want to subject her to any more trauma.

I phoned Leanne as she lived only five minutes away from the party hosts and asked if she could pick her up for me, better yet could she sleep over with her? I didn't have the heart or energy to tell Leanne what was going on at that time as I knew she would be devastated; my daughter was like her younger sister, and they just loved each other to bits.

'Please trust me and look after her for me.' I stated, trying to control the waver in my voice.

The police arrived just after 7 p.m., a male and female officer; the male officer looked so young, almost fresh out of school, with a baby face and striking blue eyes to match. With a heavy heart, I retold and relived my agonising tale again. It was past 10 p.m. when they left. They inundated me with phone numbers for Victim Support, Auckland Sexual Abuse HELP Foundation, and other agencies I had never heard of or dealt with before. I couldn't take it all in.

'A detective will be in touch soon,' they announced as they departed.

Thank God, my daughter was with Leanne as I was an emotional wreck!

I couldn't sleep that night: images of what she had endured plagued my consciousness, and then the feelings of betrayal hit me. I thought The Blackwell's were my friends. I had entrusted the one most important person in my life to them, and they not only betrayed me, but abused us both—mentally, emotionally, and physically.

It was too much to bear; no matter how I tried, I couldn't stop the hurt and pain engulfing me. I sobbed into my pillow for my baby, for her innocence robbed from her by an evil sadistic monster.

I had cruised through life without much pain or sorrow. Both my grandparents died when I was very young and were living overseas, so the impact of their deaths was cushioned by that fact, but this was so deep, so intense, I had never experienced such anguish, such pain before. The grief tormented me on a level incomprehensible to me. Somehow, somewhere during the early hours of the morning, I fell into a restless sleep.

Chapter 7

Monday morning, I had an appointment with my orthopaedic hand and wrist surgeon. My need to speak to Cathy was almost to the point of desperation, yet I knew I had to focus on my appointment. I had waited eighteen months to be reviewed, and it was really important that I attend.

As my daughter was with Leanne, I didn't have to endure the early-morning rush to get organised, get my daughter ready for school, and do the school run, which I have done for years now. I leisurely got myself ready, checking the phone every few minutes.

On the drive to my appointment, I turned the car stereo up loud so I could block out the pain which had disturbed my mental equilibrium, but it wasn't working too well.

My phone, which was situated in my jeans pocket, suddenly vibrated. Cathy immediately came to mind. I pulled over and retrieved my phone, looked at the ID caller, but private number was flashing. Deflated since I knew it wasn't Cathy, as her number was installed in my phone's memory and would have shown up on the display unit, I depressed the talk button and discovered a detective from the Child Protection Team on the line. They had booked an appointment for my daughter to attend *Puawaitahi* for a medical at 10 a.m. that morning, which clashed with my orthopaedic appointment. This sent me into a panic, as both were equally as important, yet I needed to prioritise. If I headed back to pick my daughter up from school, I would miss my appointment, and if I attended mine, by the time I drove to the school, picked her up, and tackled the rush-hour traffic over the Auckland Harbour Bridge, I wouldn't make it in time. I couldn't decide. I explained my dilemma to the detective on the phone;

understanding my situation, my daughter's appointment was left open to get there as soon as possible. Therefore, I attended mine first.

I arrived at the surgery and sat in the waiting room, counting down the minutes until my appointment. My head was spinning. Cathy still hadn't called back, and I needed to get back to the school. When my name was called out, I never heard it. I was so absorbed in my thoughts, ruminating on the events of the past forty-eight hours in my mind. I was jolted out of my trance-like state by a gentle tap on the shoulder.

The nurse started her assessment by bending and flexing my wrists and doing strength tests when once again my phone vibrated in my pocket. My phone was permanently on vibrate mode as it had gone through a full cycle wash in the washing machine a few months earlier and lost its ring tones. It was slightly annoying that I had to have it on me at all times, or I'd miss calls, but it still worked! I had promised myself a new phone but just hadn't got round to it yet. Thankfully, this time the caller ID flashed 'Cathy' calling. I felt as if I had been thrown a life raft after treading water for two days in a turbulent vast ocean desperately trying to stay afloat. The relief I felt seeing her name nearly brought me to tears. I quickly made my excuses to the nurse and answered the call.

I could hear the disbelief and pain in Cathy's voice, which was all I needed to let go of the pent-up emotions that I had been carrying throughout the weekend. I collapsed in a heap, right there in the middle of the assessment room, pleading to her to come and see me.

When Cathy arrived later that afternoon, she took me in her arms and gave me a tight hug filled with compassion. We had known each other for a little over ten months now, and we related to each other on many levels, professionally, as women, but also as mothers. I had begged her to come, but now I sat there speechless as words failed me. I was numb! I was consumed with guilt! I should have recognised the signs, they were all there—the behavioural issues, her reluctance to sleep over, the bed-wetting, her withdrawal from activities, altered eating habits, mood swings—they were all there, how could I have not seen them, but in reality how could I have known? Cathy tried to console me by taking partial blame upon herself, as she never picked up on them either, but how could I blame her? Cathy had been there for us from the start, both of us unaware of the monster that lurked nearby. But I was her mother; I should have known! Feelings of inadequacy tore through my soul. I was inconsolable!

Chapter 8

*P*uawaitahi (meaning blossoming in Unity) is based in the *Te Puaruruhau* Building (meaning sheltering the bud) and is a multi-agency centre that brings together the police and CYFS as well as Health. The health component of the multi-agency centre is the Child Protection Team for StarShip Children's Hospital. Many moons ago, I had worked at StarShip Children's Hospital on their Acute Admissions Ward and held many fond memories of my time there, but this was far from a happy occasion. Now, I was there for my daughter's internal medical examination.

I was so upset that she was going to be subjected to this as she lay on the examination table. I recalled the numerous times when I had been in the same position during my cervical smear tests, feeling humiliated and exposed, but knowing it was necessary.

The nurses were fantastic, chatting away to us, using distraction therapy, putting us both at ease and, in no time, it was done. Oh! My poor brave baby, but she took it all in her stride, not really understanding the seriousness of what was happening.

That evening, we cuddled up on the sofa together while I watched the news: an article on a rape case was being discussed by the news presenter.

'*What does rape mean, Mummy?*' my daughter asked.

'*Something really bad,*' I replied.

'*Is it like what Cameron did to me?*' she questioned.

'*Yes,*' I said, '*He has done something really bad and will be punished for it.*'

'*Will Cameron be punished too?*' she questioned me.

'*Yes, he will,*' I stated as I cradled her in my arms. I tried to explain to her the best I could.

'It's like when you are naughty and have done something bad, Mummy punishes you or puts you in time out. It's no different for adults. If they do something bad, or hurt another person, they will be punished too and sent to prison, which is a bit like time out for adults, but they are not allowed home.'

'OK,' she said, seemingly satisfied with my answer.

I looked down at her and in that instant knew everything had changed.

She was no more my little baby; her perception of her world was no longer full of innocence and fun but tainted with dark evil horrors that no child should ever experience!

The following Monday, we were back at *Te Puaruruhau*, this time for her video interview. *Puawaitahi* also work in partnership with the Criminal Investigation Branch CIB of the Child Protection Team and have a specialist team of investigators who arrange for the child or young person to be evidentially interviewed with special emphasis on the comfort and needs of the child in a safe and secure environment.

The CIB were very efficient. They also arranged for my daughter to see an ACC child counsellor on a weekly basis, and her sessions were to start immediately. ACC also provides funding for counselling services for sexually abused children in New Zealand through their Sensitive Claims Unit.

Cathy was present with me at my daughter's video interview for moral support and a student social worker who had been assigned to our case was also present.

The student social worker was a mere slip of a girl with peroxide blonde hair and nose ring, not a comforting image to a mother already highly stressed and anxious. She had a look of a grudge university student, scruffy young and immature, in my opinion. I took an instant dislike to her.

They wouldn't allow me in the interview room with my daughter or to watch her on the TV monitors; in fact, she wasn't allowed any support person in with her. I pleaded with them to let me in, but they stood firm with their policy.

My daughter was interviewed for nearly two hours, during which I had to sit outside and listen to Cathy and the fake blonde exchange stories of their social work student days. God! I wished they'd shut up, it was mindless dribble!

I just stared out of the window and tried to mentally block them out. That two hours dragged on and on as the verbal banter continued between my two supporters until finally the doors which had held my daughter captive opened, and she rushed out into my arms.

We all needed to de-stress, the one thing I knew that would accomplish that was food! I did not drink alcohol, smoke, or indulged in any illegal substances or drugs which was a blessing really, as I think I would have been a raving alcoholic-fag-ash-Lill by now, but I did have one vice—I loved my food. I wasn't overly obese as I tried to maintain my weight with years of yo-yo dieting, but I was carrying a few extra kilograms. The consensus was good old Burger King. With Cathy in tow, we headed back across Auckland Harbour Bridge for lunch as the Sky Tower, dominating over the city, receded in the background.

The next few days were a never-ending barrage of phone calls from multiple agencies, police, CYFS, and social workers. Another detective came round and took down my police statement on her laptop. I gave her an accurate account of how we met the Blackwell family and our social history together, nearly two years' worth of evidence. The portable printer that the detective was using ran out of paper; it was an exhausting afternoon!

Other than Cathy, I hadn't discussed my daughter's disclosure with any of my personal friends. I was sure they would blame me and accuse me of neglect by putting her in that situation: already I was guilt-ridden! I lay in bed night after night, blaming myself. I had put my need for some *me* time before my daughter. I had brushed aside the time she expressed her recent dislike for Cameron, which I had put down to the fact that he had disciplined her on the previous visit as the girls had fought over something trivial and she had been slightly verbally aggressive towards his daughters. I never heard her silent cries for help.

Numerous emotions ricocheted through me as I wept for the mother that I should have been!

Chapter 9

Mary was my longest friend here in New Zealand, a midwife and a single mother from South Africa; we met during a night shift at Auckland City Hospital on the maternity ward, where we were both working. We clicked straight away; I had found out that it was a week away from her birthday, and she had booked a weekend retreat for herself and her fourteen-year-old daughter over in The Coromandel. The Coromandel Pininsula is 55 kilometres west of Auckland and can be seen clearly from the city in fine weather. My fortieth was also fast approaching three days after her birthday, so me being me, I invited myself along for the trip, and our friendship grew from that moment on.

I knew I had to talk to her about my daughter. I needed some sisterly love and comfort. Mary lived over the other side of Auckland Harbour Bridge in Howick East Auckland; it was a drive in itself, especially during rush hour, but when I called her, she came over straight away. We talked and cried together, held each other, and I was comforted by her. I realised that I hadn't eaten for nearly two days and not much prior to that, I was deathly pale, and Mary had picked up on it.

We ordered in some pizzas, and I soon found my appetite as the aroma of hot pepperoni, tomato, and melted cheese hit my olfactory senses. We settled down each on our respective sofas, balancing our plate of food on our laps. Just as I was about to bite into my first slice of pizza, Mozzarella cheese strings tantalisingly hanging off the edges, the phone rang.

Little did I know that the police that morning had been round to Cameron's home, arrested him on one count of sexual violation and three counts of sexual misconduct with a minor, processed, taken to court, and released out on bail with strict bail conditions: one being he wasn't allowed to live at home till the police had ascertained whether his two daughters were at risk, and two, he was to have no contact with myself or my daughter. Obviously Mia had been by his side the whole way through, and now home alone without him and unable to come to terms with the facts, needed to lash out at someone, she needed to vent all her anger out on me.

Before I had even placed the phone to my ear to say Hello, I could hear the rage being emitted through the airspace between us. I knew Mia's voice so well, how many times had we talked over the phone talking about the girls, men, and general topics of interest that women discuss! How many times had we discussed plans and activities for the girls! I recognised her voice immediately but not soon enough as her venomous words stung my ears. I slammed the receiver down into its cradle but the damage was already done; if she was attempting to intimidate me, she had succeeded. I was shaking all over as she had caught me off guard!

With Mary's support, I managed to calm down enough to contact the police and notify them of her call. That was the last time I heard from her until the court case was heard.

Weeks had passed since the allegations were made, and I hadn't heard from either one of them. I had been on edge ever since the disclosure. I had never felt the need to confront them as I believed my daughter wholeheartedly, and I wasn't up for a confrontation with them; I had put my trust in the police to deal with him to the fullest extent of the law; however, I was concerned that they might turn up on my doorstep, looking for answers, so I locked myself in the house. I become a prisoner in my own home; every time the phone rang or there was a knock at the door, fear would flood adrenaline into my bloodstream, rendering me helpless and full of dread. I was petrified!

They knew my daughter's school, and I had visions of him turning up there to try and question her, I had to eliminate all possible avenues of contact, so I called the school, instructing them that under no circumstances was anyone allowed to pick her up from school or talk to her on the phone other than myself. At this point, I didn't feel it necessary to inform them about this harrowing situation. All in all, I was a nervous wreck!

Chapter 10

As efficient as CIB was, I couldn't say the same for CYFS. They had damaged beyond repair the most crucial part of our evidence as far as I was concerned; CYFS had approached Cameron's daughters' school as per protocol to interview the girls prior to the parent's knowledge to obtain non-corrupted statements from them. However, the school principal refused them access without parental consent, so CYFS went away with their tails between their legs; they had every right to be allowed access to the girls, but they never pressured their case forward. CYFS then approached Cameron and Mia directly for consent, alerting them to the allegations made. Instinctively, they refused to allow the girls to be interviewed.

It was two weeks later, when CYFS went in again. Two weeks was long enough to plant seeds of doubt into little girls' minds! I was furious! And yes, when interviewed, the girls contradicted my daughter's statement of them witnessing their father engaged in inappropriate behaviour with her.

I tried to keep it together, but I was struggling mentally and emotionally. I knew I needed additional help. Cathy was an ever-constant strength for me, making home visits on a weekly basis, and as much as I valued and respected her, I knew she couldn't help me on this as my issues were now psychological.

I searched frantically for the *Auckland Sexual Abuse* HELP *24-Hour Hotline number (HELP 24-Hour Hotline)*, which I had been given weeks ago by the police and found it scribbled on the back of my dairy.

The HELP *24-Hour Hotline* is a free service, providing advice and support to carers and parents of abused children. I needed to talk to someone. I waited till my daughter was in bed fast asleep before I made my call. I was diverted to an answering machine where I left my name and number and prayed that they would call back soon. Later that evening, I spoke to the duty counsellor, who arranged a crisis meeting for me the following week.

I experienced my first panic attack that weekend. My daughter and I had gone to Albany Shopping Mall to browse around the shops, not out to buy anything specific, we just enjoyed strolling round the shops together, followed by a coffee and a shared muffin. Seeing a sale advertised for *K-Mart* we popped in for a quick look. My daughter made her way to the toy aisle while I browsed the ladies' clothes, with her ever in my sight.

I don't know how or why, but for no reason I suddenly started feeling light-headed and dizzy, my heart was racing, sweat was pouring off me, I could feel it damp and clammy under my armpits. I suddenly felt my bowels contract and my breath came in waves of short bursts as a wave of terror engulfed me. I had no idea what was happening to me; all I knew was that I had to get out of the Mall. I raced towards the toy aisle, grabbed my daughter, scaring her in the process, and headed for the door. People were staring at us as we rushed past them, heading towards the car park. Outside, it was pouring down with rain; I didn't stop to put the hoods up on our jackets. I just ran straight out into the onslaught. Panic stricken, I couldn't remember where I parked the car. Usually, my daughter and I, once parked, we would notice what letter we were in as they were alphabetically zoned and come up with a name so we would remember the car's location, but it wouldn't come to mind! Rain lashed down on us, as we raced up and down the aisles, frenzied in search of my car, my anxiety levels had reached critical point. I was on the verge of hysteria: my daughter, scared and confused, not understanding why I was acting this way, even I didn't understand, all I knew was that I needed to get home! Home was safe; home was a non-threatening haven for me, not that I had been threatened in the Mall. I didn't understand it or knew why but in that moment in time I just needed to get home.

I honestly don't remember the drive home that day, though I recall being frightened and not feeling safe.

That night I was stricken by another panic attack; this time I was on edge, dizzy, and short of breath, my thoughts were jumping all over the place. I couldn't focus on one thing; my concentration was severely impaired. Although I had a crisis meeting scheduled for the following week, I needed help now; the HELP *24-Hour Hotline* was available, so I called them again.

I started using the HELP *24-Hour Hotline* regularly for advice and support. The counsellors soon became a lifeline and comfort to me, especially in the early hours of the morning when sleep wouldn't come.

At home, I was present physically, but I was mentally numb and detached, nothing felt real any more. I was still consumed with fear and panic every time the phone rang, thinking Mia would call again. I decided to purchase a caller ID phone with an answering machine so I could screen my calls.

The next few weeks passed in a swirl of activities; there was an ever-constant stream of calls from the police with updates and appointments for one thing or another to attend to. I was still having weekly physiotherapy for my shoulder and hand therapy for my wrist. I had a typical nurses' back, so I was having chiropractic sessions too. I had met up with the duty counsellor during my crisis session with the *Auckland Sexual Abuse* HELP Foundation (HELP) and now was having weekly counselling sessions with Amanda, one of their therapists, and with Cathy's visits, my week was pretty much full.

Chapter 11

The courts at first moved very fast; our case was due to come before the court on the 17 July 2009. I didn't have to attend, but I sat at home, biting my nails, waiting for the police to phone back with the outcome and also I was ready for Mia if she decided to call again.

The phone call came through late afternoon from the victim advisor, who informed me of the due process and explained that the courts were full to capacity and going through some procedural changes; therefore, the hearing would not likely be till mid to late of the following year. I was dumbfounded; to go through months and months of counselling only to be brought to the courts to relive it again was barbaric to me. I was also concerned for my daughter's mental state; although she had given her video evidence, there was no guarantee that she wouldn't be taking the stand.

Cameron was back in court several times over the next few months for predispositions, depositions, and again to decide where the trial would take place. The powers-that-be needed to decide whether the case was to be held in the High Court or the District Court due to the sheer volume of cases waiting to be heard. After a decision had been made, he was back in court again to set a date!

Why couldn't they just sort out when, where, and how in one sitting?

I was so frustrated as each court date put me on edge for the whole day, anxiously waiting until I got word from the victim advisor of each outcome. It was hell!

One of the topics discussed with Cathy at great length was so painful and traumatic to me, as I didn't have a means to go through with it, was to phone my Mum in the UK and tell her about my daughter's abuse.

I couldn't bring myself to tell her as I knew she would be beyond devastated; my girl was her baby. Mum was there throughout my labour, and she was the first person to hold her. She practically raised her single-handed from birth till we left the UK for New Zealand. My daughter, as a toddler, would always go to Grandma first before me; they had a special grandma-granddaughter relationship, and the thought of Mum being in so much pain, thousands of miles away, and not being there to comfort her was agonising for me.

I also hadn't spoken to Rebecca about it yet.

Rebecca was my daughter's godmother. She and I are very close. She is also my first cousin living over in Canada. I could talk to her about anything and everything without reservation or judgement; there was nothing about my life Rebecca didn't know about, but this was different. I was still reeling in my own emotions trying to make some sense of it all without taking anybody else's on board too. I tried to explain myself and how I felt to Cathy through the tears, sobs, and countless tissues scrunched up in a pile at my feet. I saw her eyes glisten with tears as she fought to control herself, and them from overflowing, and after a long discussion, with the compassion, and understanding of a mother herself, she gave me the inspiration and strength to make that call.

It was just as heartbreaking as I knew it would be. I waited till 2 a.m., with the UK time difference being twelve hours behind, I knew Mum would be watching her midafternoon soap opera on TV. Mum was very predictable in that way and I also wanted to talk to her before my father strolled in from the pub, half drunk. Since his retirement that year, he was in the pub more often than he was at home.

Summoning as much inner strength I could muster, I diligently dialled the number I knew off by heart and just as quick put it down, losing my nerve and courage in that one swift motion. I waited a full half hour and then tried again. I heard the connecting tone as my heart beat faster; the line was now ringing, my palms slippery with sweat, the ringing sounded so far away but yet so near, it was picked up to a deep husky voice with a monotone grunt. Instinctively, I slammed the phone down with rage! It was my father that picked up!

'*What on earth was he doing at home?*' I cried out to myself. I was sent into a panic, not knowing what to do next! I had spent an hour with Cathy, hours psyching myself up, just for him to undo it all!

'*No!*' I chastised myself. I had to do it now; it was now or never!

I decided to text Mum first to let her know I'd be calling in five minutes, and she was to take the phone upstairs to her bedroom because I needed to talk.

Five minutes later, her world was turned upside down!

Chapter 12

My friend Leanne was one in a million, a born-again Christian with a love for kids. We met in the March of that year when she set up the after-school programme on Thursdays and Fridays at the local church.

I myself was raised in a Catholic household; I attended Mass with my family until I reached the age of eighteen years. I had watched my father for many years go to church every Sunday morning, then straight to the pub, which was conveniently situated across the road from the church, while Mum, my sister, brother, and I returned home to prepare the Sunday dinner. Mum spent hours slaving away in the kitchen for my father to come home drunk from the pub and start his verbal assault on her. This was a regular feature throughout my childhood. I soon started questioning the Catholic faith and religion as a whole and came to the conclusion that the whole religion thing was hypocritical. My relationship with God ended on my eighteenth birthday.

The after-school programme was, as I found out that day, a Christian-based programme filled with games and fun activities with a Christian theme. I wasn't sure how I felt about that at first, but I found Leanne warm and welcoming. As most of the children were from my daughter's school and she was keen to attend, I signed her up. Little did I know that a beautiful friendship would spring from that meeting!

As the months went by, prior to my daughter's abuse, Leanne and I spent many afternoons together bonding and cementing our friendship. She never once pushed her faith onto me, but her relationship with God was very evident. This rubbed off on my daughter, and soon she was regularly attending the BeachHaven Anglican Church Sunday Service where Leanne ran the Sunday Bible School.

Every Sunday, I would drop my daughter off at the church and go home to await Leanne's text message to inform me that the service was over so I could go back and pick her up. Just as Leanne and I had formed a solid foundation to our relationship, they too had formed a special friendship, almost like sisters: she later became a valuable mentor and role model for my daughter.

After her disclosure, my daughter became very confused, as God was a significant other in her life by then, and she couldn't understand why God had allowed this to happen to her. These were questions I couldn't answer, I felt so helpless, so inadequate, not only had I failed to protect her but also I couldn't help her spiritually! I turned to Leanne seeking wisdom and counsel as the topic was so alien to me!

I explained to Leanne that I hadn't set foot in a church in over twenty-two years. I never prayed at night and never read the Bible; my faith was practically non-existent, and I was on unfamiliar ground. My emotional state was very fragile by then, and I cried uncontrollably. Leanne asked if she could pray for me. '*Why not?*' I thought. '*I've got nothing else to lose.*'

Already stripped of my dignity and self-worth, she prayed for us both.

Leanne and I later agreed that she would have my daughter for the weekend to discuss these issues and try and provide some answers the best she could to give my daughter some peace of mind in the knowledge that God has a plan for her, and he will always be there to love and protect her.

I thought about that statement and the cynic in me questioned the validity of her beliefs, which I personally found hard to accept. Its theology being, children are supposed to be God's little angels Made 'in His own image' to love and protect, so where the bloody hell was *he* when Cameron was abusing my daughter?

Why allow such evil upon the earth!

If God really existed, I would have some hard questions for him!

Chapter 13

As an avid reader I have read thousands of books over the years, and the previous year Mary had lent me a book, titled *Out of the Black Shadows*, by Stephen Lungu. He was abandoned by both his parents at the age of seven, and he became a violent street gang leader as a teenager. Stephen Lungu was a very bitter man against God, a concept I was all too familiar with. His book is a heartfelt account of his life, a very sad life, but through struggle and adversity, he overcame his demons and became an international team leader preaching throughout the world, especially in countries like New Zealand, which support African Enterprise. Reading his book, I was in awe of his plight with an intensity that moved me to tears. Inspired, I took strength from his struggle and contemplated my predicament in a new light.

In early October 2008, Leanne mentioned that a guest speaker was coming to church on 16 October as part of his New Zealand tour to spread the love of God; as you can imagine, I was not interested. She continued to divulge into his background when suddenly it sounded all too familiar—Stephen Lungu! Of course, *'I've read his book,'* I announced.

Evoked by the feelings of inspiration I felt while reading it, feeling depressed and pessimistic at the start of the book, by the time I had reached the last page, I was left feeling uplifted and encouraged as I walked his journey of sheer will and determination to change his life around. I remembered being in awe and full of admiration! Now the man himself was coming to BeachHaven: I was in rapturous delight. How could I not attend?

The 16 October came around fast and a small group had gathered at the church. They had set up a play area at the back for the kids while the adults took their places in the allotted seats. I sat on the last row of seats as always, too intimidated and shy to sit at the front. Stephen's presence was very commanding; he captivated his audience through humour and jest. I found myself totally engaged with him, almost spellbound. Then very subtly, he changed course and began to preach.

By this time I was enthralled. He asked everyone present to think about their own pains, struggles, and hardships, and immediately my mind wandered to my daughter; I was on the brink of tears.

'*We must allow ourselves to cry when in pain,*' he bellowed '*as unshed tears are like poison to the body, and they eat you from within.*' At that very moment, I sensed his eyes fall upon me.

I felt as if he knew me and was talking directly to me. I'm not sure how or what happened to me next, but I suddenly felt a soft warm breeze blow over me, soft enough to tickle my senses, which was bizarre as it had started to rain outside earlier and all windows and doors were shut, but I definitely felt it! I was never much of a crier, that good old British stiff upper lip was a wall I hid behind throughout my life, but that night as I sat thinking about Stephen Lungu, I started to cry; his words about tears being poisonous hit home with a ferociousness and frenzy that scared me! I cried for my daughter. I cried for myself, and I cried for years of pent-up emotions I had been carrying all this time. It was 3 a.m. when my sobbing eventually subsided, and I fell into a disturbed sleep.

The next morning, with dark heavy rings under my eyes, I woke with this feeling of enlightenment.

Christ! What happened to me last night? I felt different! No words could describe how I felt that morning, but something about me had changed, and I had no idea what! I called Leanne and arranged to meet for a coffee that morning and proceeded to try and explain myself to her; the smile on her face got wider and wider as I struggled to put it into words. The more frustrated I got, the bigger her smile; it was as if the Cheshire Cat was sitting in front of me with its big cheesy grin.

'*You were touched by the Holy Spirit,*' she declared.

'*Get out of it,*' I replied, not taking onboard a word she said.

Then she said, '*The hand of God came to you and touched your soul.*'

Now she was freaking me out with all her God nonsense, and with that ringing in my ears, we gave each other a hug as I left to get on with my day.

Over the next few weeks, I experienced some strange and unexplained events; they were very subtle at first: it started one afternoon when I was driving behind this shocking pink car, which you just couldn't miss on Auckland Harbour Bridge, stuck in a traffic jam, on the way to the city. I remember noticing the car sticker with some religious phrase slapped on its bumper. Then I started seeing things, things I would not necessarily have noticed before, like billboards with religious slogans and invites to church services or Bible study posters; they all started popping out at me. One evening, I had set my VCR to record a programme I followed on a weekly basis, but somehow, I had recorded a lady called Joyce Myer instead, (Joyce Myer is a Christian preacher who has her own Ministry and TV slot) which was really freaky as it was on a totally different channel than the one I thought I had preset. It almost felt like an invisible hand had guided me there.

I phoned Mary and asked to borrow Stephen Lungu's book to read again. This time round the book spoke volumes to me.

One evening, while in bed, reading, I had this overwhelming desire to write. I had never written anything substantial before, besides essays, back in my high-school days but, surprisingly as soon as I put pen to paper, words flowed out of me like a volcano erupting! That night I wrote my testimony! *Searching* (although I didn't realise it at the time)! I had always known or felt that I was placed on this earth for a reason, not merely to exist but for a purpose bigger than myself, but it was the what, when, and how that I didn't know; I just knew I would know when *it* found me.

Searching

My life journey has been a series of trials and tribulations, joys and sorrows, failures and achievements, forever searching for inner peace, self-love and to be!

Along my path, I encountered friends and foe, individuals that lifted me and others that put me down. I travelled to many countries, experiencing cultures so different from my own, language barriers that were soon overcome, and sights and sounds that enthralled and excited me.

But I searched in vain.

My passion for nursing found me caring for the young and old, the sick and the dying, giving so much of myself sometimes without thanks, acknowledgement, or appreciation.

And yet I searched.

One day a dear friend approached me, despondent with her own life, suggested a working holiday in New Zealand.

Excited by the prospect of spending our days lounging on the beach, I packed my bags, unaware that day that my life journey was embarking on a new path.

Not just to another country or cultural experience but to life!
Parenthood was my biggest blessing but still I felt incomplete.
My inner peace, self-love, and just being was not fulfilled.
I felt empty and alone.

My search continued.

Then one day, I came across a young lady, a mere acquaintance at first, an Evangelist by the name of Leanne, in fear of receiving a lecture I kept her at arms' length as I felt uncomfortable in her presence.

But inexplicably to me, I was drawn closer to her.

She later informed me that a visiting preacher called Stephen Lungu was in New Zealand the following week, appearing at the local church and invited me to attend (coincidentally I had read his book the previous year, so I decided to go). Little did I know my life would be turned upside down that night, as it was that night I experienced/believed that there was a higher power greater than myself at play.

I was forty-one years old.

It was then that I understood that as I had stumbled along with my life journey, searching, a presence had always been there beside me, guiding and loving, holding and supporting, teaching and moulding me into the person that I am today, sharing the highs and the lows, clearing the path for me to be exactly where I am supposed to be today.

My search is over, but the journey continues!

Paige Walker, 2008.

Chapter 14

The half-term break was around the corner, and my daughter's behaviour had intensified. I didn't know how I was going to manage. The nightmares had started. Some nights I would hear her thrashing around in her bed, screaming out to her demons in her sleep. They became so frequent that on many occasions in the morning, I would find her asleep on the floor, as sleeping in bed became a trigger for her.

Cathy had graciously organised with Barnardos for my daughter to attend the YMCA holiday camp in Waiwera for a week, Cathy knew the gravity of my situation and understood the struggle and amount of stress I was under, and a break was exactly what we both needed; her empathy and compassion was her biggest asset. I had the utmost respect for her.

I never really knew or realised how depressed I was. I had always been the strong silent type, dealing with whatever adversity that was thrown my way and coming out the other end basically unscathed, but this was out of my realm, and I had no coping skills or mechanisms to deal with it. The guilt, the betrayal, the fear for my daughter's future, my anger, self-blame, my sense of powerlessness, and the emotional strain—all had a profound effect on me.

Friday, 10 July 2009

My daughter had been at the YMCA camp for a week, and that Friday afternoon I was heading to Waiwera to pick her up. YMCA Waiwera Lodge sits on the edge of the Waiwera River, north of Auckland, right across from Wenderholm Regional Park. Kayaking, the beach, and Waiwera Hot Thermal Pools are some of the highlights at Waiwera Lodge, and it was only a forty-minute drive from home. I had set out early, and having plenty of time, I decided to take the back roads. It was a longer route but more scenic than the motorway drive. Driving along with the windows down and the music turned up, I was looking forward to seeing my daughter, when all of a sudden I had this overwhelming desire to crash the car. The feeling stayed with me for a few seconds, long enough to frighten me, and I had to pull over. I couldn't focus; my thoughts were a blur, and I couldn't get a grip of what had just transpired. I sat there trembling, confused and very scared!

The feeling passed, but in my mind's eye, the car crash, my death, the effects my early departure from this world had on my loved ones played out as if I was having an out-of-body experience and watching it all unfold. I couldn't understand what was happening to me. The drive back home with my daughter in the car was the most frightening experience I had ever encountered: the desire to crash the car versus keeping it on the road and getting home safely was a constant threat.

That same night, after my daughter had gone to bed, I found myself thinking how sweet it would be to take a handful of pills and fall asleep, never to wake up! Post-surgery, I had been given adequate amounts of analgesics for pain relief; some were morphine based and quite potent. I placed them all on the bed; there was Tramadol, Voltaren, Panadol, Codeine, and my sleeping tablets Temazepam, which had recently been prescribed by my GP as I was struggling with sleep, plenty to knock me out! I stared at them for the longest time, but I couldn't do it. I wanted to so badly, but something held me back. I knew then that I needed help. I called the HELP *24-Hour Hotline*, and I talked it through with the after-hours' duty counsellor, who advised me to visit my GP the next day.

That was my introduction to antidepressants and my mental health illness.

Panic and anxiety attacks became a frequent visitor over the next few months, but with help from my counsellor, who provided me with some tools, I managed them effectively. However, the suicidal tendencies had become a problem. Another incident occurred while I was out, shopping at Glenfield Mall with my daughter: on the way back to the car, I had an overwhelming desire to throw myself into the path of the oncoming cars; the fact that they were only doing ten miles an hour, circling, looking for parking space wasn't a factor, the desire was there.

The suicidal thoughts upset me the most; I didn't want to die. I had everything to live for. Yes, my life had been abruptly diverted onto an unknown path, but that didn't mean I wanted to throw in the towel; it wasn't me, just like these dark and ugly thoughts, it just wasn't me!

Another disturbing issue for me was that one day as I brushed my teeth, I viewed myself in the vanity mirror above the sink and suddenly had a strong compulsion to shave off my hair; I still didn't quite get it. Being of the old school of thought, despite nursing in the twenty-first century, for me depression and mental illness came with a stigma, one I found very hard to accept and identify with but was forced to as I was diagnosed with PTSD (Post Traumatic Stress Disorder and Depression), which lasted well into the following year.

October 2009 crept swiftly upon me, and I still had the *Il Divo* Concert tickets, which had weighed heavily on my mind. I had waited all year to see them live in concert, but now there was an empty void! My heart wasn't into it as it left a reminder of what had passed. As the date drew nearer, so did my anxiety levels. I didn't know if Mia would ring to claim her half of the tickets.

I became paranoid and jumpy every time the phone rang.

The ticket value was two-hundred-fifty-dollars. As Mia hadn't called, and it was a shame to waste them, I asked my daughter if she would like to go with me. She had a broad taste in music but leaned more to the Hip Hop, Rap scene, and I didn't think Pop Opera was to her liking; however, I thought an introduction to an alternative type of music would do her good. But she surprised me and wanted to go. So that evening we headed to the city towards the Vectra Arena, looking for parking nearby. Already a large crowd had gathered outside the main entrance, the air electrified from the buzz of excited middle-aged couples, my daughter must have been the youngest person there. I was proud of her and that she was still young enough to want to be seen out in public with me as a day will come when she will see me as an embarrassment, so gripping her little hand tighter in mine, we made our way inside to find our seats.

The grandiosity of the arena itself was breathtaking as if seen for the first time; though it wasn't that long ago, in happier times, we had been there to watch the Disney Princesses on Ice Tour. Memories of that afternoon flooded back to me like a cinematic reel playing out frame by frame. I am not sure if my daughter remembered the last time we were here with the Blackwell family or if she had blocked it out, but I was thankful that it wasn't mentioned. Suddenly an invisible voice boomed out for people to take their places as the show was to begin in five minutes. My daughter squeezed my hand.

'Are you excited, Mum?' she asked.

'Yes, darling,' I replied; there was no need to ask her if she was, it was written all over her face.

As the orchestra stuck its first chord, the lights dimmed to thunderous applause.

Il Divo, were a group of handpicked artists from around the world by Simon Cowell from American Idol. Following two sold out world tours, twenty-two million albums and thirty-six number ones around the world, *Il Divo* were playing for the first time in New Zealand. Their music was a crossover of Pop and Opera; it was beautiful, breathtaking, and emotionally moving.

They had just finished singing *Unbreak My Heart* (one of my personal favourites) to a rapturous applause, when the next song which was called *Mama* and dedicated to all the mothers in the audience started, my daughter looked over to me with tears in her eyes and said,

'This one's for you, Mum.'

I wrapped my arm around her, resting it on the back of her seat, and as the song went into full chorus, I could feel the rise and fall of her chest as unashamedly she cried, overcome with emotion. I tried not to notice her as I battled to keep my own emotions under control. I thought of Mia and how circumstances had brought my daughter and I together that night, mother and daughter emotionally bound together as one entity, a moment so precious burnt forever in my memory, like a Kodak moment never to be forgotten.

Chapter 15

Over a period of time, my depression stabilised on medication, and I was coping the best I could. Cathy's visits continued to give me strength and encouragement. I went to my counselling sessions with trepidation as the topics of conversation sometimes were too much for me to deal with. On one occasion I had a panic attack in one of the sessions while confronting my issues, but I still attended weekly.

I went in search of a support group, as I felt the need to connect with other mothers going through the same experiences I was. Knowing that I was not alone might have proved therapeutic. I contacted numerous organisations associated with child sexual abuse in the hope that they could refer me to an up and running group in my area: *Home and Family, Shine, Community Coordinators* for Glenfield, Northcote, and Albany areas, *Parent Trust.* I asked Cathy at *Barnardos,* Amanda at *HELP, North Shore Women's Centre, WOTS in Waitakere, Raeburn House,* and *The Rape Prevention Education Centre,* but my search was in vain.

I was constantly being advised of survivor groups for women who had been abused as children, which was of no help to me as I was specifically looking for groups for parents of sexually abused children.

There was nothing in the Auckland region.

It surely was an eye opener for me as New Zealand has one of the highest statistics of reported child abuse in the world; around one in four girls and one in ten boys in New Zealand have experienced sexual abuse. Recorded by domestic/family violence and not one single support organisation for parents of sexually abused children existed; it was shameful!

I don't know when I started thinking of setting up my own support group, but the drive and desire was there.

I Googled the Internet for information on how to start up a support group and found plenty of sites which I read eagerly.

I approached Cathy with my idea, who listened excitedly as I outlined my vision. My problem was that although I was passionate about the concept, I didn't have the knowledge or means to go about it. I did my research but soon came to realise that with no funding or resources, it would be an uphill battle. I needed to go under the umbrella of an already established reputable organisation. On her next visit, Cathy informed me that Raeburn House was holding a seminar on *Community Development*; it was to run over two half days at twenty-dollars per session.

Raeburn House is a community development organisation promoting mental health and community well-being, providing support, resources, and information.

What were the odds of that seminar, running exactly when I needed more input and guidance, coincidence, or was it a sign of things to come?

I called Raeburn House to book my place and spoke to one of their coordinators, giving her a general view of my vision for setting up a support group and my reasons for attending the seminar. To my surprise, I was invited to Raeburn House for an informal meeting.

The meeting took place in one of their rooms used for group gatherings, unventilated with a small window, catching minimal natural light, with chairs placed in a semicircular position around a whiteboard, it felt too formal and clinical for what I had in mind, but it was early days yet.

As we discussed my vision for the group, we brainstormed its attributes, strengths, and weaknesses; finally she announced that Raeburn House would like to sponsor my project with full access to their facilities! She even threw in the seminar for free, and I was elated!

We arranged to get together in the New Year to put down a plan and strategise on how to organise and promote it. For the first time in months, I felt a ray of sunshine trying to find its way through darkened clouds giving me a glimmer of light and hope, accompanied with a smile with genuine happiness behind it. However, by the New Year, I was so depressed and despondent, I never made the call.

I attended the seminar the following week. The other attendants there were a mixed group from various community organisations, including Connect Supporting Recovery whom I had never heard of.

Connect Supporting Recovery is a service that builds mutual relationships that inspire hope and encourage people to move towards their aspirations by making choices within the wider community. I took great interest in them and managed to corner their team leader during the coffee break and get some leaflets and her card.

Chapter 16

Leanne was one the closest friends I had. With most of the others, my contact had dwindled down to an occasional text except for Mary, who understood my need to be left alone, but was always there waiting in the wings to love and support me when I needed it. Although Leanne possessed a strength, which I leant on, she also was having issues of her own; her ongoing battle with immigration over the past year had come to a final conclusion, and she was heading back to Tonga to be with her husband. At the back of my mind, I knew it would come to this eventually, but the shock of it, when she told me, still caught me off balance. She broke the news to me over coffee one afternoon.

We were at *The Coffee Club* in Milford Mall, the din of ever-constant shoppers, heavy in the background, and as I listened to her, I became oblivious to my surroundings as her news washed over me. As much as I was happy for her to be reunited with her husband, a selfish part of me was devastated. I was falling apart by the seams; nothing in my life was real to me any more. I relied heavily on the few friends I had left for support, the one constant thing in my very unstable life, and now even that was crumbling.

I was deeply distressed!

The next few weeks were the hardest for me; I spent as much time as possible with Leanne, just hanging out, going out for coffee, and helping her finalise all the little things that needed to be done before she left, knowing that each passing day brought her nearer to her departure date.

The day she left, I was overcome by an immense sadness. The drive to the airport was filled with light-hearted banter between Leanne and my daughter, but for me, words failed me, as I struggled to come to grips with losing my dearest friend. Our last goodbyes outside the departure gate at Auckland

International Airport were filled with hugs, kisses, and promises of visiting Tonga in the New Year. No one wanted to be the first to breakdown and cry. We all tried to stayed strong, but for my daughter, it all was too much for her to bear; as her friend and mentor waved her final goodbye to us and disappeared into the secured area for departing passengers only, my daughter broke down and cried.

Chapter 17

28 September 2009

The half-term break was upon me again; I had been dreading it for weeks. Cathy had tried to get funding for my daughter to go to the YMCA camp again, but Barnardos declined the application, and I couldn't afford the fees to send her there myself.

(Since then the YMCA in Auckland has established the Youth Scholarship Fund to help disadvantaged young people in the community who have a keen and evident desire to be involved in a YMCA programme and where participation in that programme will provide long-term benefits to the individual and/or their family, which I have since applied for and used when in need of some respite.)

The thought of having to entertain her for the two whole weeks threw me in a state of panic and set off my anxiety attacks again.

I was struggling with the everyday things.

On top of my depression, my daughter's behaviour had become even more challenging. Every day was a battle: we fought, we argued, we were at loggerheads with everything, we just couldn't get along, and our home had turned into a verbal war zone. The two weeks passed in a frenzied state of verbal tennis, back and forth, hit for hit we fought it out.

The weekend before school was to resume, my daughter took ill; she woke up one morning, coughing, which soon turned into a chesty cough producing slimy green plugs of mucus. I was beside myself. Frantically I administered couch medicine and liquid Panadol, which I had in my medicine cabinet, to try and alleviate and relieve her symptoms as she was going to school Monday morning!

As much as I loved my daughter, I desperately needed some alone time, but alas, my efforts were in vain.

I took her to the doctor's on Monday morning, where she was found to have a raging temperature and a chest infection. The doctor signed her off school for another five days, with antibiotics, plenty of fluids, and regular Panadol. As he was relaying this to me, I wanted to cry. I could feel the tears welling up; already having endured two weeks school holidays, I was to have her at home for another week. I was crushed!

My *me time* just flew out the window!

On the drive home, I felt myself sinking to an all new low!

My daughter spent most of the week in bed sleeping, and while awake, we spent the hours watching DVDs together. The nurse in me kicked into automatic pilot as I attended to her physical needs, but emotionally, I was an empty shell as I began to disassociate!

I soon became quite isolated, rarely leaving the house except for scheduled appointments. I was still going for physiotherapy for my shoulder and hand therapy for my right wrist under ACC, which had been progressing really well.

My third and final surgery to my left wrist was booked for 11 November 2009, which just so happened to be the same date Cameron was due back in court.

ACC was in the midst of restructuring their organisation. Many complaints and protests had been lodged against the cutbacks, so I followed its progress on the news with interest since the sexual abuse cases were their primary targets and could potentially have a direct effect on my daughter's case. But the direct effect the cutbacks had on me personally and what was yet to come threw me into a downward spiral, into the pit of my worst nightmare, totally unexpected and unprepared.

Just when I felt things couldn't get any worse, I received a phone call from my case manager at ACC with the news that sent me over the edge into an abyss so deep and profound that the battle that I had been fighting was now lost with no foreseeable recovery.

The powers-that-be at ACC had reviewed my case and found that they had mistakenly approved my case two years ago, then, my injury was classified as a 'personal injury caused by a work-related gradual process' and now they claimed that my injury was caused by a degenerate disease and no longer qualify for ACC benefits and was revoking it effective immediately. This included my physiotherapy, hand therapy, my up and coming surgery, which had now been cancelled, and my benefit payments too. I was advised to seek financial aid with WINZ (Work and Income New Zealand) and was left holding the phone dumbfounded!

Reeling in shock, my brain ceased to function; a void engulfed me killing all my senses. Unable to think, see, or feel, I sat staring at the blank wall like an empty canvas awaiting and welcoming new life, but I had nothing to give. Eventually, as the numbness wore off, I couldn't help myself. I sobbed into my pillow, trying to mask the sounds of my broken spirit. I had had so many curve balls thrown my way, blow after blow depriving me of a life I once lived, the Paige I remembered no longer existed; instead, there stood a fractured woman, struggling alone on a broken road with no means of reaching her destination!

I turned to Cathy, but she wasn't in her office, so I left a heartbreaking message for her on her work mobile phone, pleading to get in touch ASAP.

With no income, and medically unfit to work, I had no other option but to go to WINZ the next day and apply for the DPB (Domestic Purposes Benefit) as a solo parent.

Chapter 18

Revoking my ACC claim was the last straw for me, and with that, things had finally come to a head. I had been pushed beyond my mental, emotional, and physical limits. My situation with ACC, my daughter's abuse, my depression, and Leanne leaving had all taken its toll. I went head first into a major meltdown. My life was a disaster zone! I fell apart under the enormous pressures I had endured over the past six months.

Cathy, having retrieved my phone message came to see me, and I broke down in front of her, unable to contain my pain and anguish any longer. I had held out for as long as I possibly could, but the weight of my circumstances was too heavy to bear any longer.

'*You need to fight them,*' she kept telling me.

But I didn't have an ounce of energy left in me to fight back; everything I had, had been stripped from me: my self-worth, my self-respect, and dignity. I was depressed, despondent, and dejected!

'*I give up,*' I declared as I held my hands up in defeat.

Because what was the use? A big corporation like ACC had all the power to do as they pleased, and who was I to go up against their decision? I was in bad way, not only had I become a liability to myself but also to my daughter as my suicidal thoughts plagued me once again.

Cathy was so concerned about my mental well-being that she proposed contacting CYFS to place my daughter in care so I could get some rest. However, contacting CYFS was not an option for me as I had been informed that CYFS preferred to place children with a family member first, and as her biological father was living nearby, there was no way I was going to hand her over to a total stranger regardless of his status; if no biological family member was available, the next preference would be foster care. Again that was not an option for me, especially considering my fragile mental and emotional state, as my depression and mental deterioration had reached the point of increased risk of possible physical harm to myself or her, I believed once in the system, my daughter would be lost to me. Anyway, my Mum was visiting again soon. I just had to hold out and keep it together until she arrived, then she could take up some of the pressure. But Mum's arrival was still six weeks away, and I couldn't keep up the pretence of coping any longer.

My relationship with my daughter was severely damaged, and if no measures were put in place at this point, it could be damaged beyond repair, so the only option I had left was for her to stay with a friend for a few weeks till I could sort myself out.

After dropping my daughter off at school the next morning, I visited my GP, where my antidepressants were increased. I then went to my friend Megan's workplace at the crèche and told her about my circumstances with ACC and WINZ. It was agreed that she would have my daughter indefinitely until I was physically, mentally, and emotionally well enough to look after her again.

I omitted the sexual abuse, unsure how much I could trust her with that sensitive piece of information. I left feeling slightly relieved, knowing I would have some time to myself to regroup, figure things out, and get that much-needed help.

Thoughts of my daughter's recent behaviours started bothering me again— the lying, stealing, and inappropriate behaviours. At least, at home with me, I knew her behaviour was inappropriate but a normal reaction from the abuse. However, if this behaviour continued whilst she was with Megan, Megan wouldn't understand and, without that knowledge, could punish her unnecessarily.

After several hours of hard thinking, I realised that if Megan was having my daughter full-time for a few weeks, it was in my daughter's best interest that she was aware of the abuse, otherwise her behaviour could be misinterpreted and, with that in mind, I headed back to the crèche. Anxiety and fear crept up my body, from the roots of my feet to the top of my head. My palms were sweaty, and I could hardly speak.

We went outside to be out of hearing from the other childcare workers. My mouth opened to speak, but no words were uttered as my brain froze. Megan patiently waited for me to compose myself.

A cry from the deepest depth of my being exploded as I melted into her arms and revealed the nightmare I had been living these past six months.

That first night my daughter was away, it felt as if a huge burden had been lifted, and I now had some space to breathe and grieve, something I hadn't allowed myself to give into.

I couldn't sleep. As much as I missed her, I was sad and relieved that she was gone but thankful that she was in safe hands.

For days, I sat and cried like I had never cried before.

'*Why me?*' I asked out loud. '*What have I done to deserve this?*'

I tried to unwind to rest my exhausted brain, which had been operating on overdrive these past few weeks, but I couldn't find the switch-off button. The TV offered me no solace. I tried to relax with a book, but the words were all a blur and not making any sense to me. I tried to sleep, but I lay awake for hours as sleep wouldn't come. My eyelids were heavy and smarting from the constant flow of tears.

It never ceases to amaze me how functional the human body is: just when you think you have shed a waterfall of tears that's when the real dam bursts.

The bedside clock noisily ticked down the minutes, reverberating in the silence of the room as I lost track of time until eventually, with the aid of my prescription sleeping tablets, I fell into a drug-induced sleep only to be woken in the morning by the shrill of the phone. It was my friend Barbara with her ever cheerful,

'*Hiya mate, how ya doing?*'

I really wasn't in the mood to talk to her, and even though she sensed my reluctance, she pressed on till I told her what had transpired over the past few days.

'*I'm on my way,*' she replied.

But I really didn't want her here with me. I was emotionally exhausted and wanted to rest, but Barbara being Barbara, wouldn't take no for an answer, so I had to be firm and tell her upfront that I didn't want her or any other company right now. I just wanted to be left alone, alone to cry by myself, alone to try and understand my situation, alone just *to be!*

She, at last, got the hint.

I finally managed to sleep that night, at what time I have no idea, but I woke to the cheerful morning chorus of birds singing outside my bedroom window.

My plan was to stay in and clean. As much as I disliked household cleaning, I always found it a good distraction when I was troubled. But Barbara having been rejected the day before was not taking no for an answer and had other plans for me that day, and not having the energy to argue with her or to deal with a confrontation, it was easier to just go with the flow.

Barbara was a character I had never encountered in all of my forty-two years, but we became good friends.

We met at a parenting course run by Parent Trust. We travelled in very different circles; our paths were never meant to cross, but because of unfortunate circumstances in both our lives, they had, and I must admit most of the time I thoroughly enjoyed her company, and I did that day too.

Being alone that night, I ached for my daughter like a mother's full breast aching for her baby's suckle and welcomed release. I wanted to feel her little warm body curled up next to mine; she always liked to cuddle up or rub her legs against me, always needing that connection with me through bodily contact. Some nights it irritated me, disturbing my sleep, but tonight, I really missed that bond with her. I felt physically cut off and severed from her now as I had done after her delivery.

For nine months she had grown inside my womb, both of us connected by the umbilical cord, a bonding of two hearts and souls, coexisting in perfect harmony which was then cut and severed at birth. That's how I felt now. I remembered what Barbara had told me earlier that day:

> *'It takes the strength and love of a mother to give up her child
> in its best interest and the child's unconditional love for its mother to
> accept it.'*

With that thought, all the guilt I had carried during that month alone suddenly was released like a flock of white doves showering me with a sense of peace. Knowing now that I acted out of love, and not selfishness, was a very empowering moment. I then slipped into a dreamless slumber.

.

With a rested mind, the next morning I contacted Cathy. I decided I was going to appeal ACC's decision.

With Cathy's counsel and guidance, I contacted ACC to start review proceedings and requested an application form for appeal. ACC's decision, in my opinion, was wrong and unjustified, and I needed to put my case forward. Then I needed some heavy artillery behind me.

I remembered Leanne had gone to the local MP for support when she was trying to get her husband's application for entry to New Zealand approved.

Wondering if it was worth a try, I contacted the MP's Office in Highbury and made an appointment for them to hear my case.

I was seen by the MP's electorate agent, who was helpful and encouraging. I asked for a supporting letter to take to my appeal; they went one better and sent a letter directly to ACC, outlining the benefits of continuing with my surgery to get me back into the workforce as soon as possible as it was a waste of tax-payers money to have me sitting indefinitely on the DPB.

ACC wrote back to the MP in acknowledgement, stating that it was under investigation. A week later the Electorate Office received a response informing them that the matter had been reviewed by ACC, that their decision stood, and that my case would be put forward to an independent reviewer for appeal. They sincerely apologised for the confusion and distress the matter had understandably caused me.

I was smoking with fury when I received a forwarded copy of ACC's letter from the Electorate Office, stating 'They sincerely apologised for the confusion and distress the matter had understandably caused me.' *They had no idea!*

This made me more determined to fight their decision.

The appeal could take up to three months before it would be heard, so I contacted my surgeon and GP, requesting supporting letters to take with me, and prepared myself mentally for the appeal the best I could.

Chapter 19

T hursdays was counselling day for us both.

My daughter was six weeks into her therapy with her new counsellor, Jasmine, who was based in Highbury. We had stopped attending sessions with the previous counsellor as my daughter evidently was still very traumatised and was not ready to work through her issues at that time, but I felt she was ready now.

Usually on Thursday mornings, I would drive across the Auckland Harbour Bridge to Mount Eden for my session with Amanda at HELP and then head back to the North Shore for my daughter's session in the afternoon with Jasmine; however, today my morning was free as my counsellor Amanda was on a two-day training course, so our session had been rescheduled.

As I was still in cleaning mode, my bedroom was blitzed from top to bottom. Feeling good about myself, I went to pick my daughter up from school. I was a little apprehensive as we hadn't seen each other since the previous Tuesday when she went to stay with Megan, and I wasn't sure how she felt about her brisk change of abode.

Our meeting was frosty, to say the least, but warmed up with each passing moment. She complained about her lack of nourishment and that she had had no breakfast or lunch that day, though a friend at school had given her a stringy and a bag of chips during their midmorning break, as we still had ten minutes to kill before her session was due to start, we quickly headed to Burger King for a quick lunch. We had hardly sat down to eat when I noticed two big balls of tears rolling down her cheeks, and splashed on to her burger wrapper.

'I want to come home,' she cried. 'I don't like it at Megan's.'

My heart melted in that split second, as tempted as I was to take her home with me, I knew I needed to be strong for us both. This time apart was more for my benefit then hers; she was safe, and I needed help until I could manage again.

How do you explain that to an eight-year-old child, who needed her mother now, more than ever, but whose mother was incapable of holding down that position! She didn't and couldn't understand.

We arrived at her therapist's office, and my daughter went straight in. I dutifully sat outside and waited patiently. I took out my mobile phone and started texting friends, which was my usual occupation while waiting. Within ten minutes, Jasmine appeared at her door and asked me into her office, which was quite strange as her sessions were half-hour stints. The previous time when the session had been cut short was because Jasmine had felt my daughter's reluctance to participate was a waste of her time, but surely we had gotten past that now as her previous sessions went well or so I thought.

I stood up apprehensively, walked into Jasmine's office and sat on the sofa.

Jasmine proceeded to explain my daughter's continued reluctance to participate in her sessions with her. She felt my daughter was only coming to please me and went on to say that professionally she didn't feel that she could help her and that she wanted to refer her on to a specialist. She started to explain the role of a play therapist when I rudely interrupted saying that I knew what the role of a play therapist was and that I was a paediatric nurse and studied play therapy during my nurse training.

My blood was boiling, I felt as if she was writing my daughter off using that as an excuse. My daughter wasn't being difficult; she was traumatised for god sake!

All I heard from Jasmine was, *'Four o'clock next Thursday to discuss the referral,'* as I stormed out the door.

My head was spinning, with fear for my daughter as well as with pure anger and frustration. I had planned to spend some time with my daughter after her session. Since she was now living with Megan, I didn't get to see much of her. But I couldn't think straight; my heart was beating so fast at that point, my palms were all clammy and sweaty, and I just knew I was heading for a panic attack. I kept thinking about Amanda as her voice penetrated through the heavy shroud that clouded my being at that moment in time.

'Keep breathing! Deep breaths Paige, deep breaths!'

I didn't want to have a full meltdown in the middle of the Mall so I breathed and breathed, inhaling and exhaling to the point of near hyperventilation, and my anxiety attack eventually passed. I just had to get home, but I had yet to drop my daughter off at Megan's.

I found my car and headed straight to her house. I ushered my daughter in and quickly hugged and kissed her with my usual '*I love you,*' and retreated to the safety of my house. As I arrived home, walking up the deck to the back door, I could hear the phone ringing, with a wail of desperation and persistence as no one picked up. I quickly opened the door, threw my keys on the dining table, and ran to the bedroom, where it was still ringing in protest. I snatched up the receiver as if my life depended on it but dropped it in my haste. It bounced off the side dresser before landing on the floor. I thought it had disconnected, but I heard a voice talking back at me. I didn't recognise the voice at first; it took a few seconds before I realised it was Sue, my hand therapist from *Hands On.*

Hands On is a specialist hand-and-upper limb rehabilitation clinic where I was being treated for my wrist injury.

Just when I thought things couldn't get any worse, Sue dropped another bomb shell.

ACC had declined my two previous hand therapy treatments as they had revoked my claim, and *Hands On* was sending an invoice for one-hundred-twenty-dollars to me for payment.

Dear God! I had had no income for the past two weeks and was still waiting for some kind of payment from WINZ. I explained to her that my case manager at ACC had informed me in our last conversation that all benefits were cancelled but any outstanding therapy could be completed; however, no further sessions would be approved, so why was I being billed for what I was entitled to? She advised me to call my case manager at ACC and find out, which I did the minute I put down the phone with Sue, but Sod's law, my case manager wasn't in and had left a message that he wouldn't be back in the office until the following Monday, bloody typical!

My anger and frustration was getting the better of me. I wanted to call the one person I knew I could talk to; I needed to talk to Cathy. I knew she wouldn't be at the office and that she would be long gone, home to her daughter and family, but I needed to at least leave a message, knowing she would get back in touch when she could. I was starting to panic, the pressure was suffocating me, and I desperately needed to talk to someone, anybody that understood my situation and would listen!

But it was Friday, late afternoon, Cathy would be off for the weekend, and I knew Amanda was on a training course that day and my counselling session with her wasn't until next Thursday. I also knew I couldn't wait till then, an overwhelming sense of powerlessness came over me, and I could feel myself getting more and more agitated. Sitting on the sofa, I began rocking back and forth, trying to get my brain into gear to think of something, but I had reached past the point of logical thought processes, the synapses in my brain were not connecting; everything was blurred. I stood and paced the floor.

'*Think, Paige, think.*'

I don't know how long I paced but slowly thought patterns started to emerge again as the haziness slowly dispersed until I finally saw the light, literally, Help, the *Sexual Abuse* HELP *24-Hour Hotline*, I can call and leave a message for Amanda. I didn't know if she worked on the weekend or picked up her messages, but it was worth a try.

I put the kettle on to make a cup of tea to ease my frayed nerves when the phone rang, its high-pitched shrill grating the little nerves I had left. I checked the time; it was only 4.55 p.m., if it had been nearly 6 p.m., I would have let the answering machine pick up as I hated being disturbed while watching the six o'clock news, but it was still early, so I answered the phone. It was Cathy. Thank God, she had checked her messages before leaving her workplace. She was known to leave her phone at work over the weekends, and rightly so, as she, like every other working individual, had the right to enjoy her leisure time undisturbed by manic clients like myself. Bless her; I had five minutes of her time before she clocked off, so I off-loaded just as I had done many times before and explained about ACC and *Hands On*, knowing that she couldn't do anything for me but listen. However, just talking it through with her helped.

Cathy listened patiently and then left me with some parting words of wisdom and advice as only Cathy could.

'*Just stop worrying as there is nothing you can do. It's Friday, so treat it like a normal work day. It's the end of the week, try and switch off, enjoy the weekend, take it up on Monday, and tackle things head-on again,*' she said.

Easier said than done when your whole world has caved in on you, but I knew what she was saying, and she was right. I couldn't wish the weekend away as much as I wanted to, so with that snippet of advice and all other avenues exhausted, there was nothing else to do but wait out the weekend.

The weekend passed surprisingly quickly. I decided to stay home and do the spring cleaning, which was due. Summer was literally round the corner, and Mum would be here soon, so I busied myself in some much-needed housework therapy.

I woke up Monday morning with a monster of a headache, wishing I could stay in bed safe and secure in the warmth of my duvet but knew I had to tackle today's issues. I dragged myself out of bed, had breakfast, and made my first call to my case manager at ACC to find out what was going on. Again he didn't pick up, so I left a message to call me back urgently. I felt I had waited long enough and needed some answers, so yes, it was urgent! I then tried Amanda at HELP again with no luck, so all I could do was resume the agonising wait again.

After lunch, the calls I had been patiently waiting for started to flow; first was Amanda. In a flood of tears, I told her about my agonising decision to place my daughter in Megan's care, about Jasmine, my daughter's counsellor deciding to terminate her sessions, and refer her on and so on. Unable to make an earlier appointment, she talked it through with me over the phone, and we settled on our regular Thursday appointment.

My case manager called later in the day, and we sorted that little issue out too. Feeling better with those two huge burdens dealt with, I felt a little stronger to deal with the rest of the week.

Chapter 20

Thursday came round soon enough, and I was back in the throws' of my counselling session with Amanda: as we had already discussed the issues at hand, we talked about coping strategies for myself as my panic attacks had started again. Arriving at HELP that morning, I was already on edge as I had my meeting with Jasmine, my daughter's counsellor, ahead of me.

That afternoon, with tools for coping in hand, I walked gingerly down the corridor towards Jasmine's office, my leather sneakers squeaking against the polished wooden floor with each step I took, announcing my arrival. It appeared as if she had been waiting for me, already on the defence to my pre-emptive attack, as she stood at her door and invited me in.

'*Enter at your own risk!*' came to mind as I sat on her bright yellow leather sofa. Her office usually had an air of calm and brightness about it, but today, it felt dark and menacing.

Again she outlined her reasons for terminating my daughter's sessions, which I totally disagreed with. As a trained child counsellor, I would have expected that she would have had the skills to overcome these barriers which would allow my daughter over a period of time, to open up and move forward, but she had only spent six half-hour sessions with my daughter and frankly that just didn't cut it as far as I was concerned.

Her response to that was, '*Your expectations were too high.*'

Well, with that ringing in my ears, there was nothing else left to say as I took my leave. I was tempted to file a complaint against her, but I had bigger situations to deal with, and if that was her attitude towards traumatised children in her care, her demise will be at her own hands!

For a month I stayed home alone while my daughter was taken care of. My time alone was spent in solitude: resting, reading, and catching up on some much-needed sleep. I only ventured out to attend my weekly counselling sessions and any other appointments I had. I saw my GP, who increased my antidepressants and sleeping tablets again.

The peace and tranquillity served me well, but I knew I needed some support with my depression when my daughter returned home.

Retrieving the Connect Supporting Recovery leaflets and card that I had been given from their team leader at the Community Development Seminar, I gave them a call. I explained my needs and how I had obtained their number and a meeting was set up. A colleague of theirs was going to call round with an information pack the following week, and we would proceed from there.

Also, while at home, I dealt with the police, Victim Support, ACC, and WINZ, respectively. I welcomed Cathy's regular visits and checkups, all the while, trying desperately to find another counsellor for my daughter without success. As Christmas was approaching, most of them were winding down for the festive season or not taking on any further clients.

My appointment with Connect Supporting Recovery and their Reach-Out Peer Support Service was very productive; their information pack contained a collection of biographies of all the peer support workers. I was given time to read them, contact the individual Peer Support Workers, and ask any questions I had about them and the Reach-Out Peer Support Service. I was then required to select three individuals from the information given: the first person selected would be my peer support worker, if she was not available, then my second choice would take preference, but if that person was also not available, then my third choice would prevail. I read the biographies with great interest and awe, discarding all male workers listed; my selection was based solely on female workers, with a history of depression and mothers themselves, as I felt, as mothers, they would understand and empathise with my situation, creating a natural bond and easier working relationship.

Thankfully my first choice, Jenny, was available. Jenny had two children: a twenty-two-year-old son and a fourteen-year-old daughter. She had a past history of manic depression and addiction to drugs and alcohol. She had overcome her mental illness and was now sharing her experience, strength, and hope with people like myself on their recovery journey.

Chapter 21

My WINZ benefit was finally being paid out to me, not much, just enough to pay the rent, utility bills, and put food on the table, but I didn't complain; sometimes you had to hit rock bottom to appreciate what you did have, and although at that time it felt I couldn't get any lower, it was a humbling experience.

'Contentment is not the fulfilment of what you want but the realisation of how much you already have.'

However, my concern was that Christmas was around the corner, and I had no surplus money for Christmas presents for my daughter. She was still at that tender age where Santa existed in her world. I voiced my concerns to Cathy during one of her visits. She promptly told me of a contact with whom she previously had a close working relationship with, who organised Christmas boxes for struggling families. I took her number and contacted her as soon as Cathy left.

Melissa was a vibrant, jovial community coordinator for Albany on the North Shore, who worked out of the City Impact Church offices. She inquired who referred me and wanted to know how I knew Cathy. As I relayed my situation to her over the phone, I became extremely emotional and gave her an account of my daughter's abuse and the effects it had had on us. She listened without interruption or questions, and when I had told my story, she divulged to me that she had been in a similar situation herself. To say I was gobsmacked would have been an understatement; I was flabbergasted! She then cordially invited me to meet up with her for coffee and a chat, which I accepted gratefully.

I was looking forward to meeting up with Melissa the following week, but what I wasn't aware of was, not only was her office based at the City Impact Church, she was also a church member and part of their Impact Team.

The Impact Team go out into the community four times a year and actively help the community and individuals in need.

I arrived at the church off East Coast Road and immediately was confronted by a building the size of two football pitches; it was immense! A structure to be in awe and proud of, I had never encountered a church of such magnitude: it took me a while to absorb it all and to find the reception area, which was just as lavish as the building itself. I approached the receptionist and asked to speak with Melissa. I was glad I had dressed up for the occasion as I was directed to a plush leather sofa to wait.

Melissa was as vivacious in person as she was over the phone. I warmed to her immediately. I followed her to the onsite cafe where we placed our orders. As we discussed my situation over coffee, I had a feeling of familiarity towards her. She had a warm and inviting presence about her, like an old friend greeting you with open loving arms. I found her easy to talk to until the conversation swerved dramatically into the spiritual realm.

My spiritual awareness had been awakened by my encounter with Stephen Lungu, but I never really explored it in depth; I was emotionally moved to tears as Melissa told me how her situation affected her on all levels to the point of being out of control, until she was saved. As we sat there in the cafe together, unashamed to show our true emotions, oblivious to our surroundings and its hustle and bustle, I reflected on her life journey and was grateful that, at least, my daughter already had God in her life and that hopefully her faith would be renewed to help carry her through.

My Christmas boxes arrived the following week, not just one for my daughter but one for me too. They were white boxes with ruby-red ribbons tied into multiple bows and curls of ribbon cascading off the knot, as if each purposely created, you just knew that were wrapped and handled with love!

Again I was overcome with emotion, as those boxes represented to me that I was loved and worthy. Since then, the Impact Team has helped me out on several occasions and Melissa has also helped me overcome some personal issues, she is always ready to help and advise me when needed, a true friend whom I value and have the utmost respect for, we have kept in touch ever since.

Chapter 22

T he week before Mum's arrival, my daughter was back home. I thought she would be overjoyed to be home with me, but she was quite the opposite. She was distant and aloof, so the rest of the afternoon and evening I spent quality time engaged with her till bedtime. That evening, alone with my thoughts, I sat propped up in bed with a cup of Hot Chocolate, reflecting on my day and my daughter's detachment.

Several days later, I discovered my daughter had been self-harming. I was so wrapped up in my own depression, I never really noticed my daughter's. Not only had I found out she had secretly been cutting her hair as I found clumps of hair hidden behind her vanity mirror and stashed in the bathroom cabinet but also that she had been physically harming herself. She started by pinching her skin, twisting it at the same time until the skin broke and bled, escalating to cutting herself. She admitted to straightening out a metal staple and running it over the inside of her thighs deep and hard enough to bleed and also cutting herself with the blade of a pair of scissors. On closer examination, I noticed pock marks all over the back of her hands and laceration marks on her thighs. *'How long had she been self-harmimg?'* I asked myself.

I had no idea, but from the scars present, it appeared to be a while!

I was weighed down by feelings of guilt of her neglect and became besieged with grief. In need of guidance and help with regards to my daughter's self-harming, I called the *Sexual Abuse* HELP *24-Hour Hotline* and was advised to contact my daughter's therapist ASAP. I explained to the duty counsellor that my daughter didn't have a therapist at that time, but I was actively seeking one. I was then advised to take her to my GP.

With this turn of events my panic attacks returned with increased frequency. On the Monday morning, after dropping my daughter off at school, I settled down on the sofa with a cup of coffee, ready to watch Australia's Biggest Loser, which I'd been following over the past few weeks when suddenly I became agitated and started biting my nails, which were already bitten down to the quick. I gnawed at the loose flesh till it bled. My black shroud engulfed me once again as I paced the room, trying to settle my thumping heart and confusing thoughts! I didn't have to question myself this time trying to find answers to this onset. I knew, as Mum's arrival was only two days away, the inevitable face-to-face meeting was unavoidable and my daughter's self harm plagued me; just the sheer thought of them both set me off into a panic. Although Mum knew about the sexual abuse, she had no idea how it had affected us on so many levels. I had no easy way of telling her. I ran every possible scenario in my head, each one dismissed as the pain it would convey would break Mum's heart; I had no way of delivering the news that would somehow cushion the blow!

With that realisation, I crumbled into a heap, hugging the sofa cushion and wept quietly.

I must have slipped into a restless slumber as I was soon jolted awake by the phone ringing in the distance. As I leapt off the sofa and ran to the phone, stumbling over the collection of remote controls on the floor, which must have fallen as I jumped up, just as my hand reached out for the receiver on its cradle where I had left it charging, it went off. I stared at the phone willing for it to ring again, but its silence just reverberated off the walls. At that moment, I felt so alone, cut off, and disconnected from the rest of the world as if the phone was my only link to the outside, and in its silence, the feeling of isolation surrounded me, like a lone shipwrecked survivor marooned on a desert island!

As the day progressed, my panic attacks got worse as one flowed into another like a snowball effect, getting larger with each roll until so big, it overwhelmed me to the point of desperately needing to talk to someone. Other than the HELP 24-Hour Hotline, the only other person I could call was Cathy. I played with the idea of Cathy sitting in on my discussion with my Mum for support and a moral boost then quickly shrugged that thought away. This was something I, and I alone needed to do, but I knew I didn't have the strength or courage to do it by myself. Feeling ashamed and weak I called her office; she picked up after two rings. I tried to sound happy and cheerful but emotionally strong, I was not. As soon as we started conversing, I was reduced to tears again as I tried to explain my fears to her.

Hating myself for doing it, and apologising profusely in advance, I made my request to her. Without thought, question, or hesitation, Cathy agreed, and with a quick change and rearrangement of her schedule, it was done. This sent me into another wave of emotional outburst as my gratitude and relief was heartfelt. As I was still having my weekly Tuesday appointments with her, we left the finer details until then. With Cathy's support, my daughter back home where she belonged, my world should have been right, but it wasn't; still something niggled away at me, and I couldn't quite put my finger on it, but I was feeling rattled again.

The day before Mum's arrival, I busied myself getting my daughter ready and off to school. Cathy was coming round on her scheduled weekly visit followed by Jenny, my peer support worker from Connect Supporting Recovery, so I got the vacuum out and tidied the place up a bit. I was feeling a little bit better. I opened all the windows; the sun was shining, a cool morning breeze wafted into the house, bringing with it a fresh smell of summer, which made the rooms feel light and airy, when out of the blue, thoughts of Mum plagued me again. No! No! No! I tried fighting off the images and using the breathing exercises Amanda, my counsellor, had taught me, which in the past had proved useful, but today they were having no effect!

Suddenly, thoughts of Cathy began intertwining with thoughts of Mum. I couldn't figure out what was going on—Mum/Cathy, Cathy/Mum—I was spinning in a vortex, grasping for answers, which I couldn't find. The one thought that emerged through the cloud was that I didn't want to see Cathy today. I absolutely, undeniably, didn't want her in my house today, which upset me no end. She was the one person who had stood by me and journeyed this road with me and would be there till the end so why, all of a sudden, was I feeling threatened by her? Again I had no answers, so I called HELP for some psychological insight into all of this.

The counsellor I spoke to gave me her analysis, which quite frankly went right over my head. I was apparently transferring my fear of talking to Mum on to Cathy; therefore, Cathy represented Mum. I didn't understand it, but I tried to take it on board with little success.

Soon after, Cathy's arrival was announced, with her usual bright and cheerful,

'Hiya.'

Before she even entered the doorway, I felt myself retreating, on the defence, ready for whatever my brain conjured up. In the fifteen months of knowing and working alongside Cathy, I had never lied or fabricated any information passed on to her. I had bared my soul to her, cried and exposed my vulnerability to her: no one knew me as intimately as she did, and today was no exception. Even feeling the way I was, I divulged my innermost feelings about her and my reluctance to see her that day. I could clearly see that she was upset by this imparted knowledge as she expressed how she also looked forward to her visits, but she understood my fears. After a lengthy discussion, she left, with a plan in place to come back on the Friday of that week so we could talk to Mum together.

Chapter 23

Wednesday morning of Mum's arrival, I awoke to my daughter's crying in bed next to me and complaining of a headache. She rarely complained of headaches but had been suffering with them recently as the stresses in her little life accumulated.

'*But not today, of all days,*' I silently screamed to myself! I was anxious enough and needed a clear head.

As Mum's flight wasn't due to arrive till midafternoon, I gave her some Panadol and sent her back to bed to try and sleep it off.

By 11 a.m. she was still in bed asleep and needing to get ready to head to the airport; I had to wake her up. I quietly approached the bed, where she lay curled up in the foetal position one hand tucked under her head while the other protectively cradled her favourite teddybear and gently shook her awake. As she slowly uncurled herself, sat on the edge of the bed and then stood up, she suddenly swayed sideways, falling back on to the bed with her head in her hands. A pain-felt cry was released from her as the headache, still present, gripped her, pulsating in her little head, which only she knew and felt its rage.

She was in no state to travel.

The journey to the airport was a good one-hour drive, that's in good traffic. I had to be leaving soon to allow extra time for unexpected heavy traffic or roadworks, but my daughter, still evidently in pain, was going nowhere. Of all the days to be sick!

I started to panic, trying to figure out what to do. Mum would be arriving shortly, and I needed to be at the airport, but my daughter was sick and needed me. My thought processes were a blur; my heart was pounding in my chest, my poor nails, already bitten down to the quick were being violently gnawed at again as I fought back the tears.

I called Cathy at work, knowing there was nothing she could do other than be that friendly, rational voice attached to the other end of the phone line, but she wasn't in. I was running out of time; my head was hurting, swirling around in a rip, with nowhere to go, and my daughter was crying at my side! My anxiety levels were reaching critical mass, but this was not a time for me to go into full meltdown.

I fought to control myself, a headache now residing within my temples, playing to its own beat as I reached out beyond the dark cloak enveloping me, hoping for my demons to disperse. I picked up the phone and started calling everyone and anyone that I could think of, but alas, no one was available to come over to look after her.

I was out of options; she would have to travel with me to the airport. My heart broke for her as she held her head in pain with every bump and jolt in the road causing her to cry out.

Arriving at the airport, I realised that in my panicked state, my poor daughter had missed out on breakfast and lunch, so we headed to McDonalds for a bite to eat and a much-needed coffee to calm my tattered nerves.

Not long after we had eaten, and feeling much better, my daughter perked up and for the first time that day, she was looking forward to her grandma's arrival while silently my anxiety grew more intense.

It started with palpitations, a flutter at first, and then a rapid succession of irregular heartbeats building to a heavy pounding in my ears as my heart beat escalated to a climax: I was overcome with lightheadedness, leaving me dizzy and faint. I sat down before I fell down and started inhaling and exhaling. In between breaths, I started dry heaving; the threat of regurgitating my recently digested Big Mac was very real. The nausea was so intense, I felt my legs turn to jelly. Thankfully, Mum's flight had been slightly delayed.

With each breath, the nausea slowly evaporated, leaving me weak and scared. For three consecutive days, I had experienced an attack and increased anxiety, the worst to date in frequency. I recognised that it was due to Mum's arrival, and that she was coming into an emotionally charged household without any knowledge of the events of the past six months or of the up and coming court case.

I so wished Mum wasn't coming for this six month visit; not that I didn't care for her company, I did, but I just hated the thought of her seeing me like this. Everyone saw it as a blessing, but to me, it was another responsibility adding to my existing stress. Mum is a fit and healthy seventy-year-old woman, but still anything could happen while she was here and my stress levels were already maxed out!

My concerns were, would she be strong enough to deal with the intimate details of the profound effects the trauma had had on both her granddaughter and on myself? I knew I didn't have the resources to cope with Mum's grief as well as my own *and* my daughter's.

Cathy and Amanda both told me that Mum was not my responsibility and that I needed to stop protecting her, but how could I not? This is who I am, the carer, the nurturer, the nurse: all my life I have been in that role, selflessly putting others before myself and that wasn't about to change overnight. However, I was aware that it had to change; for the first time in my life, I needed to put myself above all others or I would not get through this ordeal.

Mum's flight was finally processing, so it wouldn't be long now.

The next two days were spent forever in elated conversation, catching up with the news of family and friends back home in England, while at the back of my mind I dreaded Friday approaching as we were to have our meeting with Cathy, sitting in. I didn't know how to approach Mum with the news as I didn't want to start a conversation and get into details without Cathy present, so I left it till Friday morning, telling her Cathy was popping round for coffee.

Chapter 24

Friday morning, as 10 a.m. came round, I waited outside for Cathy's arrival. As I feared, my anxiety was written all over my face for Mum to see. Cathy came to me not with her usual effervescent '*Hiya*', but with open arms and a look of compassion. We embraced silently as I absorbed the strength of her presence.

Inviting her in, I called Mum and explained the reason why Cathy was here. Placing myself between the two of them, I didn't know how or where to start. Cathy broke the ice by explaining her role with Barnardos and her involvement with us. I had an overwhelming desire to run out the door, to flee from what I knew was about to unfold.

It was the hardest thing I had ever done; I watched Mum's face crumble and fall apart as I told her about the enormous strain my daughter and I had been under, its effects, and repercussions.

As she sobbed, I couldn't carry on; my composure was starting to fragment, I looked over to Cathy who understood my nonverbal message and picked up where I left off. Somehow, between the two of us, it was finally said. Aware that poor Mum was reeling with the shock of it all, I finally went over to her and we both hugged each other.

For me, it was a huge relief and emotional release. Six months of pain, heartache, fear, and anxiety flowed out of my body into an invisible torrent, rushing into an estuary towards oblivion, while Mum's journey was only just beginning. Over the next few weeks after Mum's arrival, I felt a degree of mental freedom, liberated and unburdened from my fear of Mum knowing the intimate details. A delirious relief consumed me, and with the festive season upon us, I embraced the distraction.

Christmas 2009 came and went in a flurry with the usual overindulgence of food, the company of friends, light-hearted conversations, more lunches, day trips out, and lazy days at home, curled up on the sofa, watching DVDs, content after having eaten a hearty meal. My exhaustion by nightfall, enabled me to drift off without much thought of the past six months or of the events that confirmed 2009 to be my *Annus Horribilis.*

After the New Year celebrations, I didn't want the festive season to end as it symbolised the return to reality and the pending issues I needed to face and deal with. Cathy and Jenny were both off work till the middle of the New Year, which left me feeling anxious without that much-needed support; however, the HELP *24-Hour Hotline* was available if needed, manned by a skeleton crew over the Christmas and New Year period. I was hoping not to need the service but also glad that it was available just in case.

Thankfully, I didn't need the HELP *Hotline* over the festive season, but there were times where I felt claustrophobic and feelings of being caged in. I was surrounded by company for weeks as the festive period progressed, company whom at times I really didn't want to be bothered with, while I was forced to make polite conversation on topics I had no remote interest in, all the while struggling deep down with the need to be by myself.

At times the need for solitude was overwhelming; just to be alone in my own space, in my own universe, and alone with my thoughts, just to *be.*

With the holiday season over, everyone was back at work. Connect Supporting Recovery was now on board, assisting me with my recovery from mental illness, and my first sessions of the New Year with both Amanda and Cathy came with bombshells I was not prepared for. In one swift motion my support system crumbled beneath me. Amanda was leaving HELP to pursue other avenues of interest, so my first session of the year with her was also my last, whilst Cathy delivered the second blow as she was being forced by management at Barnardos to close her case with us due to the overwhelming demand of clients on their waiting lists.

I was devastated as feelings of abandonment rocked me. The biggest event in my life was looming, and my lifelines were gone.

I was assured that until a new counsellor was appointed, I would still be supported by HELP.

I was introduced to Gillian, who assisted and helped prepare their clients for court. But my biggest fear was not having Cathy by my side. Cathy, who unbeknown at the time when accepting us as clients, was in for a life-changing experience that would affect her professional and personal life beyond what any text book could have ever prepared her for.

Cathy had walked this journey alongside me and anchored me through turbulent times. No words could articulate the loss I felt at not having her present; she had been there from the start, and I wanted her to see it through to the end with me, but it wasn't meant to be. I needed to express to her the measure of appreciation and respect I had for her; it needed to be said, so despondent and with a heavy heart, I sat down and put pen to paper.

Dear Barnardos,

I would like to extend warm thanks for all the support I have received throughout the year.

First of all, to the team leader, as it was with you that I started the Parent Course.

The knowledge you gave me has enabled me to review, change, and enhance my parenting skills, tough but valuable lessons that I have embraced, and will see me through my motherhood years.

Also I would like to thank the area manager for organising the YMCA camps for my daughter.

When her little life was shattered, you were there to help pick up the pieces, which allowed her to just be a kid again.

And finally, words can't describe my sincere gratitude and thanks to Cathy, family support worker, who, unbeknown at the time, took on quite the case-load when she was assigned to us!

As she walked alongside me, her dedication and work ethics, shone through like a welcoming beacon, which helped me navigate through some challenging turbulent waters.

Her vivacious personality lifted me during some of my lowest ebbs, while her kind, compassionate nature grounded me many times when I was lost and had given up hope, all the while maintaining a sense of dignity, integrity, and professionalism.

This has been a humbling experience. With humility comes peace and empowerment, in which I can only move forward and grow from. Some people come into our lives and quickly go. Some stay for a while and leave footprints on our hearts. And we are never ever the same!

Anonymous
To all Barnardos angels,
Thank You.
Paige Walker

Chapter 25

I worked alongside Gillian over the next six weeks, preparing for court and our victim-impact statements. I was informed by her that in her experience, most parents find that having their victim-impact statements read out in court and to the accused, empowering and validating. It felt good to know that our voices would be heard.

Victim-Impact Statement

My name is Paige Olivia Walker. I am forty-three years old.

I have an eight-year-old daughter.

I am a single parent.

My daughter and I moved to New Zealand six years ago from the UK in search of a better life. We fell in love with the people and lifestyle and consider New Zealand our home.

I had known Cameron and his family for eighteen months prior to my daughter's disclosure of sexual abuse by him. We met the family in Wellington while on a family vacation. Cameron has two daughters of similar ages to my daughter, and since our initial meeting, the girls became good friends and their friendship developed over a period of time. Cameron's wife, Mia, and I also became friends and together we spent a lot of our social time together. The girls went to each other's birthday parties, and we attended social functions together, e.g. The Easter Show, Disney Princess on Ice Tour, the movies, swimming, and other day trips out. Our visits were mainly on the weekends when we spent the day together, but soon the girls wanted to spend more time together; that's when the sleepovers started, but by then, I had gotten to know the family quite well and trusted them with my daughter.

I was always a confident, fun loving, bubbly person with a personality to match. I loved travelling and have visited many exotic locations, including the Seychelles, the Bahamas and Barbados, just to name a few. I have tried to have an overseas vacation each year with my daughter so she can experience the joys and wonders of different countries and cultures as I did.

Through hard work and dedication, I had a career that I loved, with a good working relationship with my colleagues. I also had a great social life and took part in many social activities. I also enjoyed the company of a close network of friends professionally and personally.

But since the disclosure, I have lost all the above and so much more as friends, unable to understand what I was going through, distanced themselves or were too uncomfortable in my presence.

Unable to work due to my mental status, my finances became very restricted. I lost my regular income to a DPB benefit from WINZ, and the Paige Walker I once was, disappeared, stripped of my dignity, integrity, and strengths and qualities that defined me as an individual, mother, carer, and friend.

I started my nursing career in 1984 as a pupil nurse, at the age at seventeen and a half years.

After a two-year course, I qualified as an enrolled nurse but soon realised that my passion was working alongside children. I then applied for the registered sick children's nursing course at the University of Manchester and after three arduous years, I qualified as a registered nurse with a diploma in Paediatric Nursing Studies.

With twenty-four years of nursing experience, I came to New Zealand as a highly qualified, experienced nurse with specialised skills in Paediatric medicine and midwifery. I have worked overseas in the UK and in New Zealand at StarShip Children's Hospital and on the postnatal wards at Auckland City Hospital as a respected, valued member of staff. I was blessed with a job that I loved, excelled at, which also challenged my passion and caring nature. New Zealand being a multicultural nation, I was involved in many different and diverse cultural families, assisting in their child's care, from admission through to discharge, with results so rewarding, words can't describe.

Since my daughter's disclosure on 5 June 2009, I have not been able to work, due to the traumatic impact this has had on me, and I won't be able to work in the foreseeable future.

Physical Injuries

The physical injuries affecting me by this event are minor in terms of the visible disability, but internally, the injuries are massive and very much more debilitating. I suffered frequent migraines to the point that the stress my brain was under became so overwhelming that it shut down in self-preservation mode, which in itself caused a number of issues.

I suffered from memory impairment. Unless you have experienced it, words can't begin to describe what it feels like; it's almost like your brain is in a hazy foggy swamp, and you're grappling to find your way through. The information is there, but it's scrambled and just out of reach; it's a very scary confusing place to be. Unable to process everyday activities, I became forgetful, angry, and frustrated. I remember going to the dentist one day and was physically unable to complete the form or write out my own name. The receptionist had to ask me the questions and fill out the forms for me. I was so humiliated!

My concentration became impaired to the point where I couldn't focus properly. I couldn't read a book or watch TV, basic activities I usually enjoyed. Then driving became an issue. I recall one incident where I found myself driving, not remembering getting into the car or where I was going! It really freaked me out, and I soon began to realise that I had become a liability to myself and that my daughter's safety was at risk. It was agreed, with the help of my social worker, that my daughter was to be removed from my care, which lasted for six weeks. That separation was more painful than any physical injury could ever inflict. The stress became so overwhelming, I started dry heaving and vomiting for no reason; the attacks would come out of the blue and last for hours at a time. My nerves were so frayed, and I then started having panic attacks. I remember my first attack, which occurred in Albany Mall. I suddenly experienced palpitations and shortness of breath. I became dizzy and light-headed; sweat was pouring off me, and I had no idea what was happening to me; I just knew I had to get out of the mall. As I ran out of the mall, I went into full meltdown in the car park in front of my daughter and many onlooking shoppers. I still don't remember how we got home that day! I still, to this day, suffer from panic and anxiety attacks and have not been able to enter Albany Mall since that day.

As a nurse, twenty-four years of lifting patients had taken its toll on me, and I had developed typical nurses' back. Prior to my daughter's disclosure, I was attending chiropractic adjustments every two weeks. As I have not been able to work since June 2009, I could not keep up with the payments and had to cancel my sessions. Subsequently, I have suffered ongoing back and neck pain from the uncorrected subluxations, for which I now have to take painkillers.

My mental injury prompted a spell of agoraphobia; I became a prisoner in my own home. The house was locked up tight, windows, doors, and curtains closed, I was even scared to answer the phone as Mia, Cameron's wife had previously rung and verbally abused me over the phone. Home was the only place where I felt safe. I was totally disengaged with the rest of the world and became very isolated. A mental health peer support worker from Connect Supporting Recovery was brought in to help me overcome my fears and support me through my recovery, which is still ongoing.

I became very noise sensitive. I would sit for hours in silence while my daughter was at school and soon became irritable when she returned. Her idle chatter and the TV background noise were unbearable, and I frequently sought out sanctuary in my bedroom, leaving her by herself. Constantly in a state of physical exhaustion, on many days my daughter was left to entertain herself as I was too tired to engage with her. This left me feeling guilty and feeling like a bad mother.

Insomnia became a real issue so I saw my GP and was prescribed sleeping tablets and antidepressants. It took awhile to adjust to the medications as the dosage was chopped and changed until I was stabilised. I suffered severe side effects, including a metallic taste in my mouth, to the point I would gag and vomit, also, my mouth became dry, cracked, and bled frequently. After long-term use, I am now addicted to Temazepam and Amitriptyline an antidepressant drug and will need to enrol in a detoxification programme with Tranx Drug and Alcohol Service Incorporated in the near future to wean myself off them.

Financial Costs

The financial cost to me has been a hard and humbling experience. I used up all my personal savings and spent my daughter's education fund that I had worked overtime for and put away for her future. I was reduced to receiving handouts from the church and food parcels from The Salvation Army, leaving me feeling ashamed and unworthy. Unable to keep up with the rent payments, I ended up at WINZ and signed on for the DPB with an advance payment so I could pay the rent on time, which I am now paying back at ten-dollars per week. I felt so ashamed, humiliated, and degraded I had worked all my life and never relied on the dole. I felt like a failure; I had failed myself and failed my daughter.

My financial costs spiralled as I struggled to survive on a benefit. I relied heavily on my credit card to buy basic necessities for my daughter while on many occasions I went without buying them. I used my credit card, knowing I was incurring credit card fees I could no longer afford to pay off, but I had no choice. Other financial costs include the following:

- Credit card maxed out
- Travel expenses to GP and visits at fifteen dollars per visit
- Medication costs, antidepressants, sleeping tablets, and pain killers
- Counselling fees
- Weekly travel costs to counselling for my daughter and me
- Travel expenses to Puawaitahi and the district courts

My lack of finances also had a direct impact on my daughter. I could no longer afford her after-school activities and had to cancel her swimming lessons, gymnastics, and after-school sports. All luxuries were stopped, movies, coffee's, McDonalds, as basic amenities became my priority, but my daughter couldn't understand our change in social standing and lashed out at me frequently when lollies and ice creams were denied.

Christmas was very hard on us, as I was unable to buy her any gifts. Again I turned to The Salvation Army and Barnardos for help. I don't think I have ever felt so depressed and powerless as I did that day, but I swallowed my pride as I wasn't going to destroy my daughter's belief in Father Christmas, and she would at least have a gift to open on Christmas Day.

Emotional Harm

The night my daughter told me about Cameron is hard to describe. I was in an emotional turmoil, shock, horror, anger, and numbness. There was no doubt in my mind that she was telling the truth as from the things she said, what he did to her, she described in graphic detail, there is no way an eight-year-old child would ever know these things unless exposed to them.

I battled with the betrayal of my so-called friends; I have never experienced so much anger towards another person. These were people I trusted, and how could they do this? I wished I had never met them. This monster had robbed my daughter of her innocence, had thrown her into an adult world well beyond her years and comprehension. She was only eight years old for God's sake! I cried for days over the loss of my baby! My daughter and I were always close and the thought of her keeping that secret from me on his say-so was devastating for me.

I now suffer with trust issues. When people are trying to be nice or kind to me, I always feel they have an alternative motive, and I am suspicious of their actions. I don't exactly know when the depression hit me; I think I slowly succumbed to it over a short period of time. I slipped into a very dark place, where I felt there was no way out. Being a non-smoker and drinker, I had no emotional outlet, so I internalised my feelings and went deeper and deeper into my black hole. After my first panic attack, I started having multiple attacks, sometimes several a day.

I was so low. I received an abusive phone call from Cameron's wife after his first arrest and became extremely anxious. I was scared they would turn up at my house; I feared that they might try and contact my daughter through school. I feared for my and her safety. I became a nervous wreck. Every phone call, every knock on the door sent me into another fit of panic. My stress levels went through the roof. I became more and more depressed. I would cry uncontrollably for hours, as I became more and more isolated and disassociated with the world around me. I lost my identity, my self-esteem, and also my will to live.

My first suicidal thought came while driving my car to Waiwera to pick my daughter up from camp. I suddenly had an overwhelming desire to put my foot down and crash the car into a wall. I was petrified, but I managed to pull over, then sat in the car, and cried like a baby. I suffered from many suicidal thoughts in various contexts from that point on. I would pick up a kitchen knife and put it to my wrist. I tried to remove the razor blades from my lady shavers, unsuccessfully. I suffered overwhelming desires to throw myself in front of cars, but my most troubling thoughts were at night, when in bed, alone.

I would arrange a multitude of painkillers on my bed and stare at them for ages, willing myself to have the courage to take them. I just kept thinking how 'sweet it would be to close my eyes and never wake up.' I realise now that I never intended to take my life; I just wanted the pain to go away!

Throughout all this, my mother in the UK was calling me frequently. I tried to hold it together and act normally over the phone as I couldn't tell her about her granddaughter; it was just too painful. I knew I had to tell her one day, but I just couldn't bring myself to. I remember, after a long conversation on the phone with her, I sat and cried for hours.

By November 2009, I was in full meltdown; my daughter was in the care of a friend, and I was at my lowest ebb. My social worker suggested for Mum to be flown over from the UK to help out. At first, I was so against it as I couldn't face her. I was depressed, suicidal, and emotionally unstable, and I didn't want

Mum to see me in this state. As time went on, I was neglecting myself. I hadn't eaten properly and had lost over 6 kg. I didn't recognise the woman staring back at me in the mirror; I had an overwhelming desire to shave off my hair: basically I was lost and needed help. It took me so much courage to pick up the phone and tell Mum, although I didn't go into details. Two weeks later, Mum arrived, and I had to explain the events of the past six months and what I had been through. I still didn't have the courage to tell her alone, so my social worker sat in, and between us, through the tears and pain, we told Mum.

Mum knew the family concerned from previous visits; she had been to their home and socialised with them. She was devastated by the news and took it really badly. I had to arrange crisis counselling sessions for her too. Not only had I to deal with my grief, I had to deal with Mum's too.

At the time of my daughter's disclosure, I had just started dating a guy I had recently met. That relationship didn't last long; even though he was kind and understanding of my situation and wanted to be a support, I couldn't bear for him to be anywhere near me. It's hard to put into words how I felt, even though it was my daughter that had suffered the abuse, I felt violated myself. I questioned if I could ever be in a normal relationship as how could I ever trust a man around my daughter again?

I saw him recently with his new girlfriend. At the time I thought to myself how lucky he was that he had moved on; life goes on, but for me, mine was cut short and ended on 5 June 2009. That night I cried for what could have been, and what I would never experience again.

As I struggled with myself, just getting through each day, my daughter had started acting out. Due to her abuse, she had become sexualised and was displaying abnormal sexual behaviours towards myself and to other children. These behaviours were becoming a problem, and at the time, I was still unaware of her abuse. I called upon my social worker for help and accessed books from the library to educate myself on her behaviour but still the problems continued.

The one thing I still battle with on a daily basis is my guilt and self-blame. As her behaviour escalated, I couldn't cope with her and relied heavily on the Blackwell family for respite care over the weekends, not realising that I was sending her time and time again into that situation! I blame myself for not listening to her when she said she didn't want to go and that she didn't like Cameron; I never listened. I placed her in a position of 'at risk' as I was too selfish to hear her cries for help because I wanted some time out for myself, and that's something I have to live with for the rest of my life.

It's nearly a year after my daughter's disclosure but the scars remain, like a wound that never heals.

*Our mother-daughter relationship has been seriously damaged due to the impact of Cameron's actions.

*I am still suffering from depression and am still on medication.

*I still suffer from panic and anxiety attacks though the suicidal tendencies have diminished.

*I can engage in the world for short periods of time; for example, I can go to the supermarket and do my shopping, but I don't feel safe unless I am at home and being out for too long can trigger a panic attack.

*I am unable to work, and I am struggling financially to raise my daughter on the DPB.

*I have incurred debts I can't repay at present.

*I have trust issues and query people's motives.

*I constantly feel vulnerable to my emotions and fear a relapse at any minute.

*My self-esteem and confidence have been battered.

*I am still under the Reach-Out Peer Support Service working towards wellness.

*I constantly fear for my daughter's safety, and as a consequence of that, she can't play outside or have any sleepovers with friends any more.

*She is within my sight at all times unless she is at school.

*I constantly suffer migraines something I never had before.

*My spirit and faith was crushed, and I questioned God's purpose.

I have tried to sum up how this has impacted on my life but these words cannot give justice to what I have been through this past year. People say to me that I need to put this behind me and move on with my life. But I ask how you do that when everything that defines you as a person has been taken from you. When I found out about the abuse, I could not, and do not, accept that this sixty-three-year-old man suddenly, after meeting my eight-year-old daughter, became a sexual predator. I personally believe many children may have come in contact with him in the past but have been too scared to speak up against him, or that he has just been bloody lucky and never got caught; however, he messed with the wrong girl this time.

I pursued this case to seek justice for my daughter and to validate our struggle. I wonder if, and I am concerned that, there may be many children out there that may have been victimised by Cameron. I feel strongly that anything less than a jail sentence would be a slap in the face. Home detention or community detention will not allow him to know and experience the loss of being a whole person, as I have. As Cameron works from home, he will be in his own environment surrounded by his family and friends. Under these circumstances nothing about his lifestyle would have changed. He must be accountable for his actions or the justice system will have failed us. I pray and hope that after a just sentencing I can seek some closure; it will never erase the pain and suffering we endured, but it will be a start on my road to recovery, and I hope that one day I will be able to smile and experience the joy of living again.

Paige Walker

Chapter 26

With Cathy gone, I was in need of a new social worker. Cathy had given me a few reputable contacts before she left, so I contacted each and every one of them, but they all had long waiting lists. I did a Google search on each one of them and finally selected Family Works, for one, they had the shortest waiting list of four months, and also because I liked their vision which is states as follows:

> Family Works supports children/tamariki and their families/ whanau to flourish and empowers families who are facing complex challenges.

And we certainly were! All I had to do now was wait until a social worker was available.

In the meantime, a new counsellor at HELP was appointed to work with me and a child psychotherapist with my daughter. I was going to be introduced to both of them on my next visit with Gillian, with counselling sessions to follow.

I attended my next session with apprehension. Would my new counsellor just expect me to simply open up and talk to her? She would have no idea what I had been through, so how could we possibly just pick up where Amanda left off?

Although my first meeting with my new counsellor Casey was pleasant enough, relationships are built on trust and that was something we needed to build over time, and it did; it took months before I felt I could open up to her, post-court, post-sentencing. All the while we danced a merry dance at each session, both aware of each other, occasionally testing the waters but never intrusive; she waited patiently till I was ready.

Court

The first day of court I was anxious but ready to face Cameron. I wanted to look him in the eye and let him know that I was a force to be reckoned with and that he literally *fucked* with the wrong woman this time. (Excuse the profanity!) I had fought one person or another over the years, people who had crossed my path, so I was in fight mode, with guns cocked and so ready for him. However, judgement day didn't come till the second day of court as the prosecutors were grilling my daughter first, which continued well into the second day.

Finally, I was called in to give evidence. I took a deep breath opened the doors and walked into the courtroom, with my head held up high. Cameron was in the dock to my left; as I passed him on my walk to the witness box, I noticed his head was bowed down. Ahead of me were the twelve jurors, twelve pairs of eyes locked on to me as I was sworn in.

The Crown Prosecutor Calls Paige Walker

Q. *'Could you please state your full name?'*
A. *'Paige Olivia Walker.'*
Q. *'And you're the defendant's mother, is that right?'*
A. *'Yes.'*
Q. *'You used to work as a nurse or are you currently working as a nurse?'*
A. *'I am a registered nurse, but I am on sick leave at the moment.'*
Q. *'How long have you worked as a nurse prior to going on sick leave?'*
A. *'Probably twenty-two to twenty-three years now.'*
Q. *'Where was your daughter born?'*
A. *'She was born in the UK.'*
Q. *'Is her birthday 25 May 2001?'*
A. *'Yes.'*
Q. *'When did you and your daughter move to New Zealand?'*
A. *'I came to New Zealand in 2003, in November by myself, and then my daughter came over with my mum in 2004.'*
Q. *'Here we are dealing with the events involving Cameron Blackwell, the accused. Do you remember when it was that you first met Cameron and his wife?'*
A. *'Yes.'*

Paige Walker

I was questioned for over an hour by Cameron's defence lawyer and the crown prosecutor. During questioning, I frequently glanced over at Cameron in the dock but not once did he raise his head; his shame and guilt was evident for all to see.

I wasn't prepared to wait around for the verdict as deliberations are unpredictable: they could be as little as an hour or take days. I left the court, went home, and waited for the phone call. The deliberations carried on until the end of the working day. I never received the call. That night I went to bed, left in an abyss of mental torture of the not knowing.

The next day I waited patiently; the first few hours dragged on and on as I waited in anticipation, when finally, just before lunch, the phone rang startling me, as a sudden surge of adrenaline flooded my system. I tried to control the shake of my hands, and with a deep breath, I answered the phone.

It was good news; the jury had deliberated all afternoon the day before and over four hours that morning and came back with a *GUILTY* verdict. He was found guilty by his peers of five out of six charges of sexual offence with a minor. I sat there numb; I was totally speechless for the first time in my life. The trauma of the past twelve months washed over me, the counselling, the tears, the struggles, the mental torture—it was worth it. Justice was passed down. I sat and cried tears of sadness and joy.

The sentencing was booked for four weeks later; Cameron was released on home detention till then. I wished now on hindsight that I had been present in the courtroom for the reading of the verdict, just to see his face when the guilty verdict was read out but nothing was going to stop me from attending the sentencing.

On the day of sentencing, I was nervous, not really knowing what to expect yet knowing that finally he will pay for his heinous crime, and I would finally find closure in this matter. The victim advisor and the crown prosecutor were awaiting my arrival. We took the elevator to Courtroom 2, where Cameron and Mia were already there, waiting to go in. The shock of seeing them intensified my already anxious state. I was escorted to a private room with the crown prosecutor to discuss the possible outcomes and reasons behind them until the victim advisor knocked on the door to inform us that they were ready for us.

I walked into the courtroom again with my head held high and took my place on the back row of seats together with the team members from *Puawaitahi* who were involved in our case. Cameron and Mia were seated to my left. The judge arrived and court was in session.

Introductions were made, submissions presented and read out, and the lawyer for the defence then started his summations.

Things started off OK as statements were read out and submissions made. The judge then described each offence in graphic detail, which I found hard to listen to: three counts of skin to skin contact where she was made to masturbate him; I knew what he had done, but hearing the words made me feel nauseated, and I started feeling light-headed as if I was going to pass out. I suddenly became dizzy from lack of oxygen as I realised I was holding my breath. I let go, took a deep breath and tried to regulate my breathing into a rhythmic pattern of deep inhaling and exhaling.

I tried to relax and breathe, but the room started spinning, and I was disorientated. I really had to fight hard to refocus; the list went on about how he had kissed her and repeatedly placed his hands down her underwear whilst, inside, I was screaming! If I had a gun on me, I surely would have had no hesitation using it because I hated him with such a passion, this monster, who had violated my baby and not once shown any remorse. When previously interviewed about his actions towards my daughter, the judge stated he said, *'No comment!'*

I was on an emotional roller coaster like a wave, I just had to ride it out. At that point, I felt surely a jail sentence would be served; then things changed. His defence lawyer started pleading his case; he really played heavily on his human rights as a father, and that being in jail would restrict access to his children, that he was sixty-three years old and wouldn't be able to cope being in jail, that he was the primary bread winner and that in going to jail, his wife couldn't meet the demands of the mortgage, so they would lose the family home, the financial and emotional stress he has been under since the allegations were made—he just went on and on.

My head was spinning.

What about my daughter's *bloody rights*?

Where was her right to have a normal childhood, the right to feel safe? Where were her rights when he was touching her? At that point, I felt I had lost it; my head was pounding, ready to explode. The judge then mentioned, and took into account, his previous sexual offence; that threw me a glimmer of hope; my heart was pounding in my ears, just maybe, maybe . . .

Then Cameron's defence lawyer played on his daughters' rights to have their father at home and to be raised by both parents and what the impact of him not being there would have on them.

Oh my gosh! I was enraged, as I mumbled some choice words to myself.

What about the impact it had on us? Did the judge not read our victim-impact statements?

After his defence lawyer finished and the crown prosecutor stated our case, it was over. The judge got to our victim-impact statement and commented how she had read my lengthy statement, she sounded very sarcastic, which angered me even more, and that Miss Walker states that since the event she hasn't been able to work and that her daughter has been seen by a child psychologist and reports having disturbing nightmares.

That was it!

What was empowering or validating about that!

I was on the verge of tears; I was devastated!

A sentence of twelve months' home detention was served, and then it was finally over. I was boiling with fury, a lousy twelve-month home detention sentence! The conviction was a sham. I wanted to scream!

The crown prosecutor and the detective from the Criminal Investigation Branch CIB walked me out, saying how pleased they were with the outcome, saying that in all his sex abuse cases this was the weakest case he had had, and to come out with a guilty verdict was beyond their expectations. Insensitive fucking bastards (again excuse the profanity, I only swear when extremely angered), but they had no idea; to them it was just a win they could celebrate and move on to the next case, but I was left with the aftermath, I was left to pick up the pieces. The victim advisor wanted to talk and debrief with me, but I just walked past her, walked out of the courts and into the street where the glare of the burning sun blinded me.

I walked aimlessly around Auckland city centre for hours. I couldn't go home; I couldn't face my Mum just yet; I needed time to compose myself.

When I finally arrived home hours later that day, I told Mum the outcome of the sentencing and that it wasn't what I wanted but was pleased with the outcome overall. At the same time, I was fighting back the tears as I couldn't tell her how I really felt; she was leaving the following week, and I didn't want her worrying about us, so I smoothed things over, for her sake.

That night, I lay in bed, depressed and wishing I was dead; twelve months from today, he will be a free man while I had the lifetime jail sentence. I didn't have the strength to carry on. I wanted to die so badly, to just fall asleep, never to wake up. Since that day of the sentencing, that's all I think about every minute of every day; I'm consumed by the idea. In the rare moments of lucidity I get, I am wracked with guilt over having these thoughts, but they are short-lived. My depression has hit a new low. I am scared, I am frightened, I am lost, and I am angry with him, his family, the judge, the justice system, and myself.

And there is not a damn thing I can do about it!

Chapter 27

M um left the following week; her departure was an emotional, teary event. It hadn't been the best six months of her life, but I was grateful for her love and support while she was here.

A year had passed since my daughter's disclosure. ACC's Sensitive Claims Department had previously informed me that my daughter was eligible for compensation, a lump sum payment, but that she would have to be assessed twelve months after the incident. I dutifully completed all the required documents and sent them off to their claims department.

A week later, I got a reply from them informing me that they could not approve my daughter's claim because ACC legislation states thus:

IPRC Act 2001, Schedule 1, Part 3, Clause 57(2): *If the claimant is under sixteen years of age and has cover for personal injury, that is a mental injury, the corporation must not assess the claimant's entitlements to lump sum compensation for the mental injury until the claimant turns sixteen years of age unless the corporation is satisfied that there are compelling reasons for assessing the claimant's entitlements earlier.*

There is no justice in this world; we needed that money now, especially as I wasn't working. I just couldn't get a break!

My ACC case was finally ready for review. While the court proceedings went ahead, I had appointed an ACC advocate to represent me and go over my appeal. I was mentally and physically exhausted, but I needed to call on all my reserves of energy to get through this hearing.

I valiantly defended my case in front of the ACC representative and reviewer, and at the end of the hearing, I was pleased with my performance.

If all fails, I knew I did the best that I could and I could live with that. The reviewer informed me that I would hear from her with her decision within twenty-eight days.

It was in God's hands now.

I sat in session after counselling session, unable to communicate with Casey. All the while anger and fury were eating me up inside like necrotizing fasciitis, a flesh-eating disease digesting me from the inside out.

Twelve bloody months! That's all I could think about. I couldn't accept it, I wasn't going to accept it, and justice wasn't served. Betrayed yet again but by the system this time, the very system that was there to protect and serve the innocent. For weeks I festered with this thought when suddenly my fighting mode suddenly kicked in, and as the saying goes,

If the mountain won't go to Mohammed, Mohammed will go to the mountain!

I suddenly felt renewed, energised; I knew what I had to do.

Amanda, my former counsellor from HELP, had told me once before during one of our therapy sessions, that win or lose the court case, I would still be able to claim damages against Cameron via civil proceedings.

No amount of money could ever replace what we had lost, but boy, Cameron hadn't heard the last of me yet.

I started phoning lawyers till I finally found someone who was prepared to listen to me and assist me with the fight I had on my hands. Unemployed, on the DPB, no assets to speak of, depressed but with enough fight in me. I found a lawyer who was willing to listen and help. As I had no fixed income or assets, our first step was to apply for legal aid. Considering that we already had a conviction, the prospect of a favourable outcome was good.

The legal aid forms were completed and sent off. While awaiting a response, my new-appointed lawyer applied to the courts for all copies of the transcripts of our case and for my daughter's video evidence.

30 June 2010

A letter to The Registrar at Auckland District Court was sent
out requesting Court Transcripts from criminal Proceedings by my
lawyer.

Request For Court Record From Criminal Proceedings

Letter

1. We act for Paige Walker who is the mother and sole
   guardian of her daughter born on May 25th 2001.
2. In about April-May 2009, her daughter was sexually
   abused by Cameron Blackwell of stated address.
3. In 2010, in Auckland District Court Cameron
   Blackwell was convicted of sexual offences against
   Miss Walker's daughter and sentenced to home
   detention.
4. Pursuant to the Privacy Act 1993, Official
   Information Act 1982 and the Criminal Proceedings
   (Access to Court Documents) Rules 2009, we request
   a full copy of the court record concerning these
   criminal proceedings. In particular, we request a
   copy of the transcript of all oral evidence given by
   her daughter, a record of Mr Blackwell's conviction
   and the sentence he was given. We request this
   because Miss Walker wishes to file a Civil Claim
   for Exemplary damages against Mr Blackwell. As she
   will be her daughter's litigation guardian, she is
   not able herself to give evidence of the sexual
   abuse. This evidence will clearly be crucial in any
   Civil proceedings.
5. We have applied for Legal Aid for Miss Walker. If
   there is a fee for obtaining the Court record,
   please advise the fee.
6. Please call the writer if you have any questions
   or if you wish the writer to come to court to copy
   the file.
7. We enclose Miss Walker's signed authority for the
   release of this information.

We just had to wait now.

Chapter 28

It wasn't long before we heard from the Legal Services Agency. I said a silent prayer as I opened the letter. I was advised that my application for legal aid had been referred to a specialist adviser for recommendation, and they would be in touch once a decision had been made. It wasn't exactly the news I wanted, but at least, at this point it hadn't been declined.

The weeks rolled by, as I anxiously waited for news on my ACC review and also to hear from legal aid. I was in a state of limbo. My trips to the letterbox were a daily source of disappointment and frustration for me. The first good news came three weeks later, my legal aid had been granted. This was quickly followed by the news that I had won my ACC review, and not only had I won my case, but ACC had to reinstate my benefits and back pay all compensation I would have received from the date of termination. As the saying goes

You wait forever for a bus, and then two come together!

I was elated! Finally, I could get off WINZ and get the much-needed surgery for my wrist. The future was suddenly looking good.

My ACC benefits were finally reinstated, and the slow progress of reassessment of my wrist commenced.

Chapter 29

I got a social worker within three and a half months, Elizabeth (Liz) from Family Works, but by then, I was struggling: the court case, its outcome, and ACC were taking its toll on me. During those months, my mental health deteriorated rapidly. I was in withdrawal from my medication. All the symptoms they were prescribed to prevent were now having an adverse effect on me; instead of counteracting the symptoms, they were increasing my depression and anxiety levels. I felt like I was literally going mad. I wouldn't cooperate or participate during counselling sessions, opting rather to sit there in silence or answer in monosyllables.

I became intolerant of most things as the withdrawals took a hold of me. My cognitive thinking and mental acuity became seriously impaired as my depression worsened. I was losing my mind!

Literally!

That's when I started hearing voices (also known as auditory hallucinations, a condition associated with depression), bombarding me with negative talk and feedback, together with the unpredictable mood swings, I turned into Mrs Jekyll and Hyde, exhibiting a classic split personality, one minute being the demonstrative loving caring mother that I was, the next, displaying uncharacteristic behaviours, including paranoia, inappropriate bursts of anger, screaming and shouting like a sergeant-major on drill patrol. Life for us both became very difficult as I became unbearable to live with and although I was conscious of my behaviour, I just couldn't stop myself. Once on the benzo withdrawal roller coaster and suffering psychosis, I couldn't get off as much as I wanted to or stop the ride.

Alone in my room, night after night, I stared blankly at the ceiling in a catatonic state for hours, unable to string together any kind of thought process until one night my suicidal thoughts kicked in again. My ideation this time involved my daughter as I wanted to free her from all the pain and hurt I had caused her. I wanted to free us both from the mental and psychological torture, anguish, and agony we were both suffering. I cried as I silently apologised to her for everything she'd been through and vowed to never allow her to be hurt again.

The thought of both of us leaving this pitiful world of evil and destruction behind was sweet sorrow, and yet as I lay there in bed formulating a plan of action, I knew I could never go through with it. Somewhere in the recess of my mind, I was able to communicate with my consciousness that it was the medication distorting my thinking, despite the voices goading me on. I knew I needed some serious help and time out. I seriously needed a break from all my stressors as I was fearful of the possibility of seriously harming myself and my daughter.

But all I could do at that time was call the HELP *24-Hour Hotline* to talk it through.

I knew I had reached crisis point and was soon referred to my local Community Mental Health Team (CMHT) I was assessed and started on a non-addictive antipsychotic drug called *Quetiapine* and monitored by the staff with daily phone calls. Unfortunately like most drugs they came with their own list of side effects of which I suffered several of them.

I had, for the past eighteen months, held up to the constant pressures of dealing with my friends' betrayal, my daughter's abuse, her behaviours, the counsellors, police, the lawyers, the court case, the individual therapists I'd been working with, and ACC, already having lost so much I now had lost my mind!

Chapter 30

(I reached a milestone and breakthrough in my therapy with Casey although I was unaware of it at the time!)

Unable to talk to Casey, I refused to attend my next counselling session and took it upon myself to find some respite care for myself. Casey called later that morning to see why I had not shown up for my session as I had attended every session previously, and it was out of character for me.

The anger, resentment, and frustration that had built up over the last few days, all fought for supremacy, my anger won as I lashed out at Casey, claiming she could no longer help me, all I was hearing week after week from her were *words, words, words* and nobody was doing anything to help me. As I was yelling at her, with venom in its wake I expressed how my daughter's behaviour was not improving despite the counselling and support she was receiving, that my counselling sessions were unproductive, my issues unresolved (all untrue as I had a fantastic support system in place, but I was in withdrawal; my head was in a completely unrealistic space in that moment in time, and I couldn't be reasoned with); basically, I was having a meltdown. She tried to be rational with me throughout my outburst, but I was having none of it; my verbal onslaught must have lasted a good twenty minutes ending with the phone being rudely slammed down, but not before I made it clear to her that, I would sort and help myself out.

The 'HELP' Foundation, emphasis on HELP yeah, right, what a joke!

I was like Mt Ruapehu, New Zealand's largest active volcano, dormant for years, when suddenly and with no warning, erupting with a ferocity so intense and violent, an unseen rage and force spewing plumes of smoke, ash and fire into the atmosphere, intensifying as it gained an inner strength.

God help anyone caught in its path of destruction.

Unfortunately Casey was caught in mine.

Once I calmed down, I planned my self-help strategy. Basically, I was going to phone every organisation listed until someone listened to me and offered me some help. So with my ultimate goal in sight, I picked up the phone and started dialling.

After several calls to agencies, I wasn't feeling as confident as I had been when I first started out. Nobody provided or had respite care facilities. I was rapidly becoming despondent.

After a few more calls, I was beside myself but I continued my quest, after searching through pages and pages of contact resources on the Internet, I came across Te Puna Whaiora Children's Health Camps.

Te Puna Whaiora Children's Health Camps is a charitable trust and non-governmental organisation offering services to children and families who are requiring support to achieve positive life outcomes whilst coping with health issues and social issues, including family breakdown, education grief and loss, social isolation, and relationship management. It collaborates with families, referral agents, and schools to assess individual needs and to develop a tailor-made care plan, setting goals with the child and family, which often include the following:

Out-of-home service provision at their residential facility for five weeks, participating in social skills and activity-based programmes, and attending their on-site school. Te Puna Whaiora translates as 'Spring of Well-being' the name was gifted to them as a reflection of their work.

I was blown away; it was just what I was looking for, but unfortunately, you couldn't self-refer; referrals had to be made by a referral agent, such as a social worker, counsellor, or school teacher.

I contacted them, again explaining my situation and requested an application form.

The following week, even though I felt pleased with myself that I had actually achieved part of my self-help goal, I attended my counselling session with Casey with trepidation and my tail between my legs. I wasn't sure how she reacted to my outburst, but I knew I had to apologise as I was totally out of order speaking to her the way I did and accusing HELP of not assisting me after everything they had done for us, getting us through the court case and ongoing therapy up to now. My behaviour had been unforgivable.

Fearful of rejection, I entered her room and was greeted with a big smile. Confused, I sat down, made myself comfortable, all the while perplexed why this woman, after having received an onslaught of verbal abuse from me, was sitting there, bright and breezy smiling at me! We talked about my explosive episode at great length whereupon Casey stated that after months of therapy, she felt we finally connected. A divide that had been present since the day we first met, at last, bridged as I opened up and expressed my innermost feelings, displaying my vulnerability and susceptibility to her instead of being the strong, hard woman I had always portrayed, tenaciously holding on to my feelings.

'*Welcome to therapy,*' she declared, grinning from ear to ear like the proverbial Cheshire Cat from Alice in Wonderland, and with that, yes, she agreed, I was at breaking point and needed some respite care. But where and how was the question? Tears pricked the back of my eyes as a sense of relief overwhelmed me; the tears turned into sobs as I sat there and unashamedly cried. Deep primal waves of grief, rocked my body as the pent-up emotions were finally released. Suddenly I felt the sofa sink with the weight of Casey sitting herself next to me embracing me like a mother comforting a wounded child. That small act of kindness sent another wave of tears flowing until they subsided all the while being held in Casey's arms. I couldn't remember the last time someone held and comforted me in that way, but in that moment, I felt safe and loved. Strangely enough, I didn't feel embarrassed or ashamed of the intimacy shared. As we parted but remaining physically and emotionally connected, I collected myself even though I was exhausted and emotionally spent.

Once composed, I informed her of my findings and explained the need for a referral for Te Puna Whaiora Children's Health Camp. She agreed to do the referral for me and set the wheels in motion. At the end of our session, I humbly apologised again for my behaviour, which she graciously accepted, and we moved on from there with a newfound respect for each other.

Later that week, I met up with Liz, my social worker from Family Works and described the events that had taken place since I last saw her. She suggested the need for a strengthening families meeting.

'*Which was what?*' I asked.

Strengthening families is a process supported by Family and Community Services, which have agreed to fund and attend strengthening family meetings as part of their work. By bringing together all agencies involved in your care, they work out together what support your family/whanau needs and what each agency is going to do. Then everyone agrees on a plan to move forward, achieving your goals, with follow-up meetings to ensure the plan is working.

It sounded good to me, but with Christmas just around the corner and organisations winding down for the festive season, how soon could this meeting be arranged and take place because I was rapidly losing my patience.

'*Leave it with me!*' I was informed, and I did.

Within days, I received a call from the coordinator of the Strengthening Families Agency, and within a week the strengthening families meeting took place at the HELP Foundation premises.

All agencies involved in our care attended: my daughter and my counsellors, liz my social worker, The Children's Health Camp were also invited but couldn't attend, they sent a message that my application was being considered and they would be in touch. And finally, for moral support, Cathy was by my side as my support person.

The meeting, I felt, went well. A plan was formulated and executed, each agency knowing their role and the support they were to provide, and a follow-up meeting was booked.

Chapter 31

I waited for four months to receive a reply from the courts informing me that our request for the court transcripts was granted and another month for confirmation that the court transcripts had been received by my lawyer.

She got on to it immediately and a letter to Cameron was sent out, outlining my intentions.

Letter to Cameron Blackwell

10 December 2010

1. We act on behalf of Paige Olivia Walker, who is the mother and sole guardian of stated, born on 25 May 2001.
2. The purpose of this letter is to notify you that Ms Walker intends to file civil proceeding as litigation guardian of her daughter who was sexually abused by you in April and May 2009 and to give you an opportunity to settle the matter prior to her filing proceedings.
3. She intends to claim $150,000 in exemplary damages for the assault and battery you committed against her daughter and for breach of fiduciary duty.
4. Ms Walker instructs that in 2009, you sexually abused her daughter as follows:
   a. On two occasions during Easter 2009, you made her daughter masturbate you;
   b. On the second of those occasions, you kissed her daughter on the mouth;

    c. On a later occasion before or on 30/31 May 2009, you touched her bottom on the skin; and

    d. During the weekend of 30/31 May 2009, you made her masturbate you.

5. In late April 2010, you were found guilty by a jury in Auckland District Court.

6. At a sentencing hearing on 21 May 2010, you were sentenced to twelve months home detention. The facts set out in paragraph 2(a) are taken from the sentencing notes of the judge, a copy of which is attached.

7. Ms Walker instructs that your sexual abuse of her daughter, who was aged seven or eight at the time, has had a devastating impact on both the daughter and herself. We refer to the victim-impact statements prepared by Ms Walker and her daughter, a copy of which is attached.

8. Since these victim-impact statements were prepared, Ms Walker instructs that her daughter's behaviour and psychological state has deteriorated. She has had ongoing behavioural problems and continues to receive regular counselling.

9. Although her daughter is covered by the Accident Compensation Act 2001 ('the act'), section 319 of that Act allows her (or her mother as her litigation guardian) to file a claim for exemplary damages despite her daughter's personal injury covered by the Act.

10. Your sexual abuse of her daughter, while she was a young child staying in your home with your wife and two daughters, was a flagrant and extremely damaging breach of trust of a vulnerable child. The jury found that your behaviour occurred on four occasions. The sentence imposed was relatively light, particularly given that the sentencing notes record that you had a previous conviction for an indecent act.

11. We consider that the sum of $150,000, at least, is warranted to mark your outrageous behaviour. The effects of your abuse are yet to be fully disclosed.

12. Ms Walker is in receipt of legal aid.

13. Please let us have your response by Monday 10 January 2011.

14. We advise you to instruct your lawyer on this matter.

Chapter 32

While my lawyer handled the legal side of things, it was time to sort myself out and come off these medications. I had been on Temazepam since my daughter's disclosure. Temazepam are known as a type of Benzodiazepine which are minor tranquillisers and highly addictive. Addiction to them can result in serious withdrawal symptoms, and I was in withdrawal.

For a while now, I had been suffering withdrawal symptoms ranging from nausea, headaches, metallic taste in my mouth, mood swings, and sensitivity to loud sounds. 2011 was fast approaching, and I wanted the New Year to be the beginning of the end of my journey.

Jenny from Connect Supporting Recovery had been working alongside me and was still assisting me with my recovery. As a mentor using the IPS Model (Intentional Peer Support Model), she helped me accept, face up to and acknowledge that the abuse is part of our lives now, mother and daughter, not just another victim in the making, but survivors, not to be denied or pretend it never happened. By acknowledging this and accepting it, we would be able to move forward, *and it was time*.

She had previously told me about Tranx Drug and Alcohol Services Incorporated and the service it provided to help wean people off drugs. I made the call and a pre-assessment meeting was set up.

Tranx Drug and Alcohol Services is a community-based addiction service that specialises in benzodiazepine detoxification and counselling. They are recognised as specialists in the field of benzodiazepine reduction and are funded to provide this service free to the community.

I was assigned to a drug counsellor, Becky, who was the loveliest person I would ever wish to meet, so down to earth, yet professional and highly skilled in her field of drug rehabilitation. She explained the detoxification programme, how it worked, how it would make me feel as I went through the transition period from Temazepam to Diazepam, the side effects I would experience and the expected outcomes.

I was keen to get started, so after some debate, she devised a programme for me to start straight away, on Christmas Day 2010 to be exact, but I didn't care; missing out on the festivities, to me, it was a small price to pay to start the journey to reclaim even an ounce of the woman I used to be.

The transition on to Diazepam took me by surprise; I knew it was going to be rough, but I wasn't prepared for the real thing.

Thankfully it had been arranged for my daughter to spend Christmas and New Year with friends in Hamilton as I didn't know how I would react to the changeover in medication. I was so grateful she wasn't around to see me.

The side effects were severe; the first two weeks were the worst: most of that time was spent in bed, half sedated or in the toilet, vomiting. The gastric reflux was painful, and I needed an antacid to help with that. Antacids work by reducing the amount of acid in the stomach, counteracting the burning sensation. I also experienced tactile hallucinations, creeping sensations on my skin. I felt as if ants were crawling all over me, in my hair, over my face, under my clothes, and in my bed. I knew it wasn't so, but the feelings were very real to me and drove me mad at times.

The headaches were the most debilitating side effect of them all. They weren't headaches as such but were described by Tranx Drug and Alcohol Services as a tight band around the head. However, I felt as if my head had been placed in a vice and slowly being squeezed as the pressure inside my head built up to the point of exploding. This pressure caused pain at the back of my eyes, which blurred my vision. It hurt to read, it hurt to watch TV, and it hurt to lie down and close my eyes; the pain was unbearable. (Imagine a migraine but ten times worse!)

Weekly visits to see Becky, my drug counsellor, assured me that all the symptoms I was experiencing were very normal and the side effects would eventually subside. I wasn't as confident as her, but I just had to go with it. Also, I was so woozy; at times, I became unsteady on my feet and suffered several falls.

One in particular, where I stretched out my left hand to break my fall but unsuccessfully landed in a heap on the floor. Several hours later, in pain in my left wrist, the same wrist I had fought and won my ACC review over recently; as I was once again covered by ACC for that wrist, I called up *Hands On* for an appointment, and lo and behold, I was back in splints again!

Chapter 33

I was blessed with a group of friends that rang to check up on me daily over the festive season and a dear friend who called in with food for me on a regular basis, but I had no appetite.

Christmas and the New Year passed in a daze, and my daughter was soon back home. Slowly, normal life resumed as all my support contacts returned to work, and yes, slowly, the side effects did abate, and what I was still experiencing was tolerable.

The 10 January 2011 came and went with no response from Cameron. While I was keen to move forward with filing a claim with the district court, my lawyer wanted to give him another week to respond. As some organisations were still on leave, it was possible his lawyer was too, so we waited.

Three weeks passed, and we still hadn't heard from him, so my lawyer started the paperwork to file a civil suit claim. I signed the affidavit and other documents required to be the litigation representative on behalf of my daughter, and if he still refused to respond, we were prepared to go ahead and apply for a judgement against him serve him and force him into bankruptcy, if need be, but one step at a time.

In the third week of January 2011, I received a call from The Children's Health Camp and was informed that my daughter had been accepted to attend camp and was to start at the beginning of the next school term, which meant I only had one week to get her organised. The Field Worker had been in touch and had arranged for my daughter and I to visit their facilities and to complete the paperwork.

The morning of my daughter's admission to The Children's Health Camp, my daughter was quite excited at the prospect of being at the camp. After the

Powhir, a beautiful Maori welcoming ceremony which includes speeches, dancing and singing performed by the staff, I settled my daughter into her dorm and with a heavy heart left her in the capable hands of the camp staff.

I was consumed with separation anxiety. We had never been apart for that length of time since she was three years old when I left her with my Mum in England while I returned to New Zealand for three months to establish myself with work and finding a suitable home for us. I was besieged with anguish and heartache leaving her behind. I struggled to hold back the tears as I drove home alone that afternoon, feeling the emptiness around me, also the guilt of wanting some respite from her, but also missing her so much.

I had to fight the desire to turn back.

That first week my daughter was gone, I came down with the worse migraine since the start of my detoxification programme, which lasted seven days; was it a combination of the drug withdrawal and the anxiety of handing my daughter over to complete strangers? I wasn't sure. I contacted Becky, my drug counsellor, at Tranx Drug and Alcohol Services, who could not shed any light on why my transition period was taking so long. I was on my sixth week, yet still I was suffering.

The next day, again miserable, fed up, feeling low, depressed with a pounding head and in tears, I called Becky back, and again she had no answers for me. In my anger and frustration, I lashed out at her; she didn't know me long enough to know or understand the level of stress I had been under this past two years. I felt she was looking at my situation purely from a physical perspective from the drug withdrawals while I believed my issues were emotional and psychological.

I missed my daughter with a renewed intensity.

At my next session with Becky, I disclosed in great detail my journey over this past two years and the toll it had taken on me; she had been aware of my daughter's abuse as that bit of information had been passed on during my pre-assessment interview and documented in my file, but she had no idea of the effects and ramifications it had had on me. With that information at hand, she took it to her supervisors where they discussed it at length, and it was agreed that possibly the detox maybe working but camouflaged under the emotional stress, which in itself could be manifesting in these debilitating headaches and migraines. So with that in mind, it was agreed to start the first reduction process and monitor the headaches.

Despite the headaches, I needed to get away, away from the city, away from everything and everybody, to a place unbeknown to others, where nobody would be able to contact me, and where I would be able to just *be*; and I knew exactly where that was, up north in Kaikohe near The Bay of Islands with my dear friend, Tiny.

I met Tiny during my first visit to New Zealand back in 1999 when I worked at StarShip Children's Hospital, and we became good friends. Throughout my early pregnancy, she was there for me and had supported me when I made the agonising decision to return to the UK. While overseas, we remained in touch until our joyous reunion when I returned to New Zealand with my daughter in 2004.

Her house had always been my second home, and whilst we remained in touch when she was living in Auckland, the visits became infrequent once she relocated up north. I was long overdue for a visit.

Tiny lived up to her name: tiny in stature, being shy of five feet tall, but what she lacked in height, she made up with a heart so big, filled with love and compassion. A friend I knew who would enjoy my company but also allow me my space to rest. With my daughter safe at camp, I made the call, packed my bags, and hit the road.

The journey up north took a little over four hours with a lunch break in Whangarei's Town Basin Marina. During those hours, as I drove further and further away from the city, my head started to clear. The counsellors, my peer support worker, my social worker, and all my other issues melted away, all left behind in Auckland. I didn't realise how weighed down I was with it all until I reached my destination.

On arrival, Tiny was there to greet me with open arms. I fell into her embrace and was wrapped with love, warmth, and safety, with the overwhelming feeling of coming home.

Over the next seven days and nights, after many hours talking with Tiny and shedding a torrent of tears, I searched for the woman I had lost. Sat on her deck overlooking the rolling hills of Ngapuhi land (Ngapuhi, is a Maori iwi or tribe located in the Northland of the North Island), the silence broken only by the singing of nearby cicadas, I finally came to realise that I could not reclaim that woman back until I had forgiven her.

For the past two years, I had held on to the fact that somehow it was my fault, and that the blame of my daughter's abuse lay firmly on my doorstep. The shame and incompetence of being a bad mother had consumed me long enough. It was time for forgiveness, to release myself from the expectations and beliefs I had adopted as my own. As I embarked on a soul-search, looking for acceptance and that I was worthy to be loved and to be forgiven, I left the Northland lighter and with a purpose.

The following day of my return home to Auckland, I was expecting Jenny from Connect Supporting Recovery to pass by, but what I was not expecting was the blow she delivered, nor was I prepared for it. The organisation had informed Jenny to start closure proceedings with me as our allotted time of twelve months was coming to an end, and therefore I only had four sessions left with her!

Perfect bloody timing, just when I needed her the most!

Jenny was as frustrated as I was. But she knew, mentally I was stronger than ever and that I was going to be OK without her support.

Even so, I was devastated!

Our last four sessions were spent on working on the strengths I had previously identified in myself and which I had utilised in times of stress and mental debilitation, and we formulated a goal plan for me to use if need be.

Our last day together was spent in reflection on how far I have come since our first meeting over a year ago. Then, a woman, broken by circumstance, desperate, and in need of help! Today, a woman who had fought vigorously for justice for her daughter, overcome adversity, empowered, and drawing on such inner strength, who was now working on reclaiming herself. I sat in awe as I reflected back on my journey with her.

Chapter 34

In May 2011, the courts finally approved my application, appointing me litigation guardian on behalf of my daughter for the purpose of conducting proceedings against Cameron, claiming exemplary damages. He had thirty working days to contest the claim, which, personally I felt, would be suicidal if he did, as the crimes listed, he had already been charged and convicted of, but would he come to the party quietly? I feared not! By the end of June 2011, Cameron's thirty days were up, and he had not filed any response, so we proceeded to prepare an interlocutory application on notice for hearing to determine and assess the amount of damages to be awarded by the courts.

By 9 August 2011, affidavits from my daughter's counsellor and The Children's Health Camp were written and sworn in, outlining the continuing effects the abuse still presented on my daughter and the challenges we continued to face because of it. The need for continuing therapeutic support and counselling for us both at least till the end of the year was emphasised, and the impact of the abuse on my daughter, as its effects would be ongoing as she progressed into puberty, adolescence, and well into her adulthood were also highlighted.

I was hoping for a hearing date soon, and surprisingly, it came through within a week of filing the application. It was set down for 12 October 2011 at 2.15 p.m. as a formal proof hearing; therefore, I had to be present at the courts for the hearing. I would probably have to take the stand and may have to answer some questions from the judge, but it all rested on what Cameron does or if he even attended.

Cameron was later served with the documents and notice of the court date hearing! This only gave him the opportunity to dispute the amount to be awarded but not his liability. If he did not attend in person, the hearing would probably be on the papers submitted and, hopefully, I wouldn't have to take the stand.

During this period I received confirmation of ACC's approval for my wrist surgery, which I had, and recovered well from, with weekly hand therapy and acupuncture with *Hands On*.

The bombshell came on Friday 7 October 2011. Five days before the case was set down to be heard, I received a voicemail from my lawyer to contact her ASAP. Her call unnerved me as I could hear the urgency in her voice. When I finally made contact with her, she informed me that she had received a call from Cameron's barrister that he was prepared to settle out of court and would I consent?

'*What the hell?*' I uttered under my breath.

I wanted my day in court, I wanted our suffering acknowledged, and I desperately wanted satisfaction of his suffering even if it was of a monetary settlement—I needed that closure!

We hadn't received one iota of correspondence from him since we filed the civil suit back in May 2011 and days out from court on a Friday afternoon when the working week was just about to close for the weekend, he springs this on us, a tactical move on his part to rattle me, and it worked!

To say I was stoical was an understatement; this last-minute diversion sent me into a full emotional tailspin. I couldn't think straight. Thoughts and words bounced around in my head, but I was unable to catch them, rearrange them, and place them into audible logical sentences.

I had prepared for weeks for this hearing. Read, and reread, the court transcripts and my victim-impact statement, compared the effects the abuse had on my daughter and I, then and now, and while there had been tangible improvements achieved with the help of therapy, the damaging effects were still very evident and very present as we continually dealt with the enormity its impact has had on our daily lives.

It robbed me of two and a half years of my life, as a mother, friend, and daughter. My daughter was robbed of two and a half years of her childhood and innocence. I suffered two and a half years of unspeakable trauma, emotional and physical stress related health issues, anger, depression, frustration, suicidal thoughts, and feelings of shame, guilt, and unworthiness. Having to go to counselling week after week, reliving the pain again and again! Attempting to articulate thoughts and feeling so alien that the strain of holding it all together brought upon endless torrents of tears of anguish and hurt so deep and primal that it scared me.

A wise woman told me once that it took two brains to think, so reflecting on her wisdom I contacted Casey at HELP for advice and to help centre me.

After much discussion with her, I was mentally beat. I was only forty-four years old but felt older as the strain of the past two and a half years had taken its toll on me.

That night I feel asleep in an exhausted heap, only to be confronted with it when I woke the next morning.

After much thought and deliberation, I consented to attempt to settle out of court. I decided to hand over the negotiations of the case to my lawyer to handle. I had faith in her, that she had our best interests at heart, and would do her best for us, as at that point I just wanted to be free of it.

My initial thoughts in pursuit of the civil case were to "*stick it to him*" and make him pay (financially), seeking my revenge in court with a hefty settlement as this reparation was not just about him or the money; it was about (or what I believed) my need to make him suffer as I had. Only then I felt that I could put this behind me and move forward; it was also about (what I thought) my personal validation and justice, which I felt had not been handed down appropriately during the initial trial and sentencing. What I didn't realise at the time was that even if all the above had been achieved, I would still be in a prison, built around my pain, anger, and rage as I unconsciously carried that resentment close to my heart suffocating my ability to grow instead of letting it go.

As quoted by Nelson Mandela, "Resentment is like drinking poison and waiting for your enemy to die."

It was just another form of *self-abuse*!

A new day brought with it a clearer head and rationality. I spent the day in quiet reflection on this journey that brought me to this moment and time. I was tired of fighting, I was tired of living in the past, and I was tired of being consumed by this dark entity that had defined me these past few years.

I had had enough!

I needed closure, I needed acceptance, I needed forgiveness. I needed to feel alive again.

I needed to be spiritually, mentally and emotional free from all the stress, strain and pressure's that I have carried these past few years so I can have peace and joy in my life once again, but most of all to reclaim *me* back, Paige Walker, the one person who hasn't been available to me or my daughter since this ordeal began. I needed to come home.

This awareness brought me to a place many people fear to go, but I knew at that point I had to visit to review and analyse my thoughts and feelings, positive and negative in the hope to grow and learn from the lessons presented to me, as wisdom is only gained by going through such experiences. I needed to do a mental cleansing, which in itself is hard to do, as one must look at oneself in truth and honesty as not to make amends and forgive oneself would have no meaning.

From an early age, as early as toddlers, some of us when emotionally harmed, physically hurt or mentally abused adopt self protecting behaviours which enable us to cope with our personal situations. We may unconsciously carry our wounds close to our hearts throughout our lives and sometimes into adulthood. This method of coping often starts in the home between family members, their family dynamics, attitudes, beliefs and perceptions can all contribute to these behaviours, but it is most often seen within sibling rivalry. If differences in the parental styles of children occurs, children may compete against each other to gain their parents attention over their sibling which can include aggressive behaviours. They learn to judge and easily lay blame on each other offending and hurting each other along the way. They quickly accuse one another if things don't go their way or adopt a victim attitude for personal gain, or, if on the receiving end of some of these acts, some children may adopt self protective behaviours just to survive or even conform to the mould imposed on them.

The purpose of both these styles of behaviour is, so that they remain in relationships with their parents or the closest person to them despite the possibility of psychologically, physical or emotional harm to them in the process.

Victimisation can also be seen in school playgrounds as clicks between the most popular and outcast students are formed, resulting in isolation of the injured party, right through to adolescence as jealousy, envy, and mistrust of peers develop as individuals find their place in the world into adulthood.

If any of us have suffered, been targeted or exposed to these negative behaviours from an early age, most of us develop coping mechanism, but some of us don't.

I now realise that at a young age, unable to cope with my circumstances I unconsciously adopted a victim mentality as many times I felt victimised so I learnt coping behaviours to survive my youth and deal with the events that transpired during that time.

Now as an adult I understand how as a child I became a victim, burying my Anger, Fear, Shame and Resentment as it was safer to do so than to fight against it. And why my old patterns of behaviour had now re-surfaced.

The little girl back then, so bubbly, vivacious and full of life, who was destined to transform from the humble caterpillar into a beautiful butterfly with a promise of something wonderful was suppressed under the all that anger, fear, shame and resentment which clipped her wings and stunted her growth.

But I wasn't a child anymore, they say that it's how you deal with adversity that defines whether you become a victim or not and I was no longer going to allow myself to be a victim, I was going to fight against it to give that beautiful butterfly a chance to grow its wings, fly and be free.

I was deep in this thought when suddenly I had an epiphany, that aha/ light bulb moment, as I soon began to realise that I had it all wrong; instead of seeing the blessings and people in my life, I had distanced myself from my friends and loved ones and embarked on a destructive path of vengeance and retribution. The hard realisation that the more I tried to punish Cameron, the more I was hurting myself hit home with such a force, which rocked me to my very core.

I had allowed the presence of evil to seep into our lives; yes, his actions or the events that occurred, I had no control over, but *I* allowed them to victimise me, which kept me a prisoner in my own hurt and pain. All this time while I had been channelling my energy into Cameron, seeking revenge, I made him my priority instead of my daughter, myself, and living.

I had lost my soul to the devil! As the Chinese proverb states,

'If you are hell-bent on revenge, dig two graves': one for your enemy and one for yourself. *And my final resting place was deep and waiting for me.*

I suddenly had the revelation that I and only I controlled my destiny, and only I had the power to change. My higher consciousness kicked into gear as I was no longer going to allow him to dictate and control my life. All that anger, rage, and pain, I would use it and give it meaning. I wanted to be that mother whom my daughter could be proud of, a role model for her, poised with dignity, integrity, and respect, in the knowledge that I did the very best I could for her but also knowing that love, grace, and compassion was the way forward, and if she grew up to be a strong, independent self-assured woman, my role as a mother would be a joyous one.

With the gift of acceptance and understanding, my heart was now open and slowly my awareness and empowerment, which had been buried for so long surfaced. As I sat with this turn of events, there and then I made the decision *to let it all go, to surrender myself to what is,* and hand it over to God to release myself from all the pain, the hurt, the guilt that consumed me.

That small act of letting go was a life-changing decision for me, it was my awakening moment!

Chapter 35

T he journey I took to arrive at this emotional release and beyond my victimhood did not transpire overnight; it had subconsciously unfolded from the moment of my daughter's disclosure till I arrived at this higher consciousness of understanding. It was a long and painful journey, one I had to live through, the pain of being victimised, to experience every overwhelming moment of hatred, to feel every explosive element of rage and suffer every terrorising moment of fear until I had nothing left to give except love and forgiveness. *Total forgiveness!*

I took a deep breath and exhaled as the weight of the past few years, which I had carried for so long was released in the awareness that my higher power had always been lying inside me, dormant, for the past forty-four years, watching and waiting for the appropriate time as to when I would be open and receptive to receive its blessings. A sense of serenity, calm, and stillness enveloped me. My soul soared in the freeing of my spirit as I sat in awe of this blessing and allowed myself to surrender to its essence. My mind drifted to the fridge magnet sitting on the fridge door, the well-known poem by Mary Stevenson, 'Footprints in the Sand.'

Footprints

One night I had a dream.
I dreamed I was walking along a beach with the Lord.
Many scenes of my life flashed across the sky.
In each scene, I noticed footprints in the sand;
Sometimes there were two sets of prints,

Other times there were one set of footprints.
This bothered me because I noticed that
During the low periods of my life,
When I was suffering from anguish,
Sorrow, or defeat,
I could see only one set of footprints.
So I said to the Lord
'You promised me, Lord, that if I follow you,
You would walk with me always.
But I have noticed that during the most
Trying periods of my life there have only
Been one set of footprints in the sand.
Why, when I needed you most you
Have not been there for me?'
The Lord replied, 'The times when you
Have seen only one set of footprints,
Is when I carried you.'

By Mary Stevenson from the original 1936 text. Copyright 1984

I had always been aware of the poem, but this was the first time I really understood it, and it had true meaning to me. In reflection, I understand now why I didn't succumb to my thoughts of suicide and self-harm, as during my darkest moments, the creator and ruler of the universe held my hand, guided me, and walked beside me through it all as it wasn't my time to depart; bigger and better things awaited me.

As I now walked in truth, humility, and grace, I began to struggle with the decision either to continue with the civil suit or discontinue the proceedings, conscious that its initial purpose was based on revenge. However, that dilemma resolved itself when several weeks later, I received a letter from my lawyer, informing me that she had received verification of Cameron's financial and home situation from his barrister, and it wasn't good news. Unaware of the price he had paid for his transgressions (of which I cannot disclose to you) he was in a situation where he was without the means to pay any amount of settlement, and I was advised to drop the case as if we continued and proceeded to judgement, the outcome would be his inevitable bankruptcy, which would be of no benefit to me.

Understanding now that everything is preordained as part of the divine plan, I believe God was tired of being ignored by me as he had been knocking on my door long enough, it was time to really make his presence felt, and this time I acknowledged and welcomed him into my life. I accept and believe that God placed Cameron in the situation that he now finds himself in, not as punishment for his actions but a humbling lesson for me to fully embrace and learn from! It was a powerful lesson of humility, grace, maturity, emotional and spiritual growth, which finally released me from my self-imposed prison and set me free.

Any money received from him would have been tainted, contaminated, and infected in pure evil, and by accepting it, I would have been just as guilty as him. So with peace in my heart, I casually walked away from the case with my dignity, integrity, and self-respect intact, true in the belief that it evolved exactly the way as it was supposed to.

I truly believe God has better plans for us; its value, not by monetary means but something far greater, though right now I don't know what it is yet, but trust that my destiny will unfurl just as it is designed to. I am at peace with my experience and the choices have made and ready to heal and move on with my life.

The only thing I needed to do now was to get word out into the wider community about Cameron, not as retribution against him but to prevent and protect another child and family going through what we did.

I had been notified by a friend about the Sensible Sentencing Trust, New Zealand Paedophile and Sex Offender's Database. The Sensible Sentencing Trust was formed in March 2001 by a small group of motivated people with a passion and a vision to help create a patriotic, crime-free New Zealand through the promotion of personal responsibility and a better deal for victims of crime.

After a thorough search of the database, I could not find any mention of Cameron listed despite him having a previous conviction. I composed an email, requesting information on how to list such a person. I received a response immediately requesting as much information as possible including the following:

- Name and address of the offender
- Legal description of, at least, the primary offence
- Date of when the offender was convicted in court
- Location of the offence

All of which I had at my finger tips. The more information they had on him, the quicker they could add his file to the database. I sent everything through so they can do a thorough check on him, and I waited to see what other skeletons he had in his closet. Within two days, I received a reply from them that a file has been composed and added to the database. He is now currently listed in the New Zealand Paedophile and sex offender database.

Conclusion

As I walked this Broken Road, I changed along the way, at times the road moved with me, at times away from me. I gained strength, wisdom, and knowledge and with that strength and wisdom, I tamed my anger, as it is only when the wisdom gained doesn't subdue the anger, that anger will destroy you, and I wasn't going to allow this experience to rob me of who I am and turn me into a bitter woman.

To date, Cameron has never shown any expression of remorse, and most likely in this lifetime, he would never admit to what he did or acknowledge his actions, but his legacy will live on through his daughters.

It's been nearly three years since my daughter's disclosure; where I was once a broken woman, today I stand tall and proud having overcome, restored, rehabilitated and whole again with life and living.

It is my belief that stricter guidelines and education for GP's need to be in place regarding the risks of long term use of Benzodiazepine and the need to closely monitor patients taking them. Benzodiazepines are usually prescribed for short-term use but are abused through lack of awareness and education. By the time I arrived at Tranx Drug and Alcohol Service Inc, I had been on them for 2 years and in sever withdrawal. I strongly believe that had my GP been aware of the risks associated with long term use and that I had been monitored and assessed while taking Temezepam, I believe my body would not have become addicted and therefore I would not have reached the stage of being in withdrawal and having to endure the horrific process of drug detoxification programme. However I am still working with Tranx Drug and Alcohol Services on my drug detox and rehabilitation programme as it nears its completion and no longer experience suicidal thoughts or ideation. Though I still suffer from tactile hallucinations, these creeping sensations linger as the residual chemicals from the Diazepam are slowly being removed from my body.

I have been discharged from The Community Mental Health Team having discontinued the Quetiapine. I still attend counselling on a weekly basis with my daughter at Auckland Sexual Abuse HELP Foundation; my mental health has improved, and I am enjoying time spent with my daughter and living again while totally committed to my healing process. We also found a church nearby, which we both attend weekly, and my daughter is actively involved in the church youth group.

I came to the point of acceptance and forgiveness with the help of my counsellor. However, giving the gift of forgiveness does not alleviate the accountability of Cameron's actions but offers him an opportunity to learn from his mistakes if he so chooses to.

But for me, I have forgiven, but I will never forget, as to forget would dishonour the journey I have been through and the lessons I have learnt along the way, which have enabled me to be the role model my daughter needs.

I think back to when I wrote my testimony 'Searching' smiling to myself, I now understand how apt my search was and its destination! Which took me to some unknown territory and some unexpected physical, emotional, and spiritual places. I now realise my life unfolded exactly as it was meant to. And now, it is time to move forward with my life.

(Readers, I most point out that coming to this higher level of consciousness was not made overnight, I really had to work hard on myself to become one with myself working through my own guilt and face my own demons, as well as shed a river of tears, to get to the point where I could love and forgive myself to receive this gift of understanding and awareness; my work towards forgiveness was even harder. Every journey begins with the first step, and the steps taken on my road to forgiveness were many, but worth it.

If any of this is resonating with you or your inner child, please seek professional advice to help you through the process as it can mentally free you from many unresolved issues you may or not be aware of.

My counsellor, Casey, lovingly and with gentle hands guided me through the process, and yes, I hit brick walls along the way and repressed memories were unleashed, but with her help, I was able to come to a point of understanding, myself, the role my inner child played in my dealing with my daughter's abuse, acceptance, and yes, forgiveness, as there is nothing too big that can't be forgiven!)

The passion and desire to start up the Parent Support Group continued to burn fire in my belly, each day growing stronger in intensity. I was mentally, physically, and spiritually stronger; I could feel my spirit driving me to reach out to the parents who resonated with my journey *as we are one*, not only here in New Zealand but around the world. It was time to live my dream, to present myself to the world as an advocate to all parents hiding behind that wall of shame, humiliation and pain, and for society to stand up and recognise the pain and hurt us parents go through and fight for adequate help and support for us. I started my quest by applying to do the victim-support-volunteer-training programme as this would put me in touch with victims where I can support them through their trauma and help guide them through the lengthy trial proceedings with the empathy and compassion they need, and knowing that *I have truly walked in their shoes.*

It has been a privilege writing this book, and I thank you for sharing this journey with me. Know you are not alone, and believe, one day you *will* smile and live again.

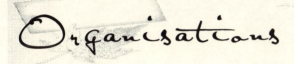

Organisations

0800 Barnardos 0800 227 627
General enquires http://www.barnardos.org.nz

Victim Support
Auckland District Court
3 Kingston Street
Auckland
New Zealand
Tel-(09)9169000
Fax-(09)9169010 Criminal
Fax-(09)9169046 Family
Fax-(09)9169047 Civil

Auckland Sexual Abuse Help Foundation
24 Hrs Hotline
Tel-(09)6231700

Puawaitahi Multi Agency Services
99 Grafton Road
Auckland
New Zealand
Tel-(09)3072860

Paige Walker

Variety, the Children's Charity
209 Great South Road
PO Box 17276
Greenlane
Auckland 1546
New Zealand
Tel: +64 9 520 411
Fax: +64 9 520 1122
Email: helpkids@variety.org.nz

Home And Family
2A Seaview Ave
Off Onewa Road
Northcote
North Shore
Auckland
New Zealand
Tel-(09)4199853

Tranx Drug and Alcohol Service Incorporation
Second Floor, La Gonda Building,
203 Karangahape Road,
Po Box 68-701
Newton
Auckland
New Zealand
Tel-(09) 3567305
Fax-(09) 3567315
Email: tranx@tranx.org.nz

Community Coordinator
Birkenhead /Northcote
Tel-(09)4868400 Ext. 8854

Community Coordinator
Glenfield
Tel-(09)4868400 Ext. 8786

Community Coordinator
Albany
Tel-(09)4770300

Nelson Mandela Quotes (Author of *Long Walk to Freedom*)

Sensible Sentencing Trust
0900 Safenz (723369)
http://www.safe-nz.org.nz/

Northshore Women's Centre
5 Mayfield Road
Glenfield
Auckland
New Zealand
Tel-(09)4444618

Parent Trust
13 Maidstone St
Youthline House
Grey Lynn
Auckland
New Zealand
Tel-(09)3760400

Raeburn House
138 Shakespeare Road
Milford
North Shore 0748
Auckland
New Zealand
Tel-09 486 8939
Tel-09 441 8989
Fax-09 441 8988
Web: www.raeburnhouse.org.nz

Paige Walker

Family Works
Private Bag 150, Albany Village
North Shore
Auckland
New Zealand
Tel-(09)4482633
Fax-(09)4158073
Web: www.familyworks.org.nz

WATS
Waitakere Abuse and Trauma Service
Auckland
New Zealand
Tel-(09)8372491

YMCA Waiwera Lodge,
Po Box 54,
Waiwera 0950
New Zealand
Ph-427 9219 Fax: 09 427 9241
Email: waiwera@nzymca.com

ACC
Po Box 1426
Wellington
New Zealand
Freephone 0800735566
www.acc.co.nz

The ACC Act 1972

Strengthening Families
(Birkenhead Northcote Glenfield Branch)
Tel-(09)4803109
http://www.strengtheningfamilies.govt.nz/

Te Puna Whaiora Children's Health Camp
Pakuranga Branch
1-9 Pigeon Mountain Road
Half Moon Bay
Manukau 2012
Auckland
New Zealand
Tel-(09) 5344017
Fax-(09) 5374885

Rape Prevention
Po Box 78 307
Grey Lynn
Auckland
New Zealand
Tel-(09 360 4001)
Fax-(093604014

Crisis Line
Tel-(09)3604004

Legal Services Agency
Po Box 1576
Rotorua 3040
New Zealand

Connect Supporting Recovery
215 Wairau Road
Glenfield
North Shore
Auckland 0745
New Zealand
Tel-(09)4433700

African Enterprise www.africanenterprise.co.nz

Paige Walker

City Impact Church
794 East Coast Road
Albany
North Shore 0630
Auckland
New Zealand
Tel-0800 Church

www.footprints-inthe-sand.com

Electorate Agent to Dr Jonathan Coleman
MP for Northcote 15 Rawene Road
Birkenhead Auckland
New Zealand
Tel-09 4198021
Fax-09 419 8025

Community Mental Health Team
44 Taharoto Road Takapuna
Private Bag 93503
North Shore 0740
Auckland
New Zealand
TEL-09 4871414
Fax-09 4871424
(Emergency A/HRS-09 486890

www.areyouok.org.nz

Acknowledgements

Amazing grace! How sweet the sound that saved a wretch like me.
I once was lost but now I'm found, was blind but now I see.

(John Newton, Published in 1779)

Many angels walked this journey alongside me, protecting, supporting, and guiding me throughout, my appreciation and gratitude is boundless to you all.

Cathy, you were there with me at the beginning and with me till the end. Without your support, especially in those early days, I would not be here today, *I thank you*.

To Jenny, my mental health peer support worker from Connect Supporting Recovery, your patience and understanding of my highs and lows never ceased to amaze me; without judgement or expectation, you helped me reach my goals while lifting me up during some of my lowest times. *I thank you.*

To Casey, my counsellor at HELP, I have to smile when I think of you and our sessions together; we danced a merry dance around the houses for quite some time as I tried to avoid any form of emotional connection with you, but with gentle hands, patience, and understanding, you guided me to a point where I was able to relate and move through my anger and pain to a place of awareness and personal enlightenment, which has made me a better woman and mother. I look forward to continuing my healing with you. Where previously I attended our sessions full of fear and trepidation, now I am open to receive the lessons and fully embark on my spiritual and emotional healing to wellness. I am and will be forever indebted to you and the HELP Foundation. *I thank you.*

To my dearest friend Mary, you stood by me when others walked away, unable to deal with the issues at hand. I am blessed to have such a friend in you. Love you heaps, girlfriend. *I thank you.*

To Melissa, you have been a tower of strength to me from the day we first met. Thank you for your compassion, prayers, and encouragement. I finally understood and embraced the lesson you were trying to teach me. *I thank you.*

To Becky at Tranx Drug and Alcohol Services, when I hit those low points during my rehabilitation and projected my anger and frustration on to you, you never gave up on me, you had faith in me even during the times when I wanted to give up, you believed and trusted that I would rise above it all and see the beauty in myself; it has been an amazing journey with you. *I thank you.*

To my beautiful daughter, God has a divine plan and a wonderful future for you; he gave you the strength and courage to endure the path he has bestowed on to you, and he will never forsake you or leave your side. I hope that one day you will see the blessings and lessons that God has gifted to you and that you continue praising and thanking him as you reap your earthly rewards until you return to him. *I thank you* for being the best daughter a mother could ever have.

And finally, I would like to acknowledge all the unmentioned angels who was there for me, no matter how big or small a role you all played in my life journey, you were always nearby; this book is dedicated to you all, as without you all, this book would have never been written.

I thank you all.

With love always,
Paige